SANTA ANA PUBLIC LIBRARY

D0407104

REMAKING ITALY
IN THE
TWENTIETH CENTURY

Critical Issues in History

Series Editor: Donald T. Critchlow

REMAKING ITALY
IN THE
TWENTIETH CENTURY

Roy Palmer Domenico

ROWMAN & LITTLEFIELD PUBLISHERS, INC.
Lanham • Boulder • New York • Oxford

ROWMAN & LITTLEFIELD PUBLISHERS, INC.

Published in the United States of America
by Rowman & Littlefield Publishers, Inc.
A Member of the Rowman & Littlefield Publishing Group
4720 Boston Way, Lanham, Maryland 20706
www.rowmanlittlefield.com

12 Hid's Copse Road
Cumnor Hill, Oxford OX2 9JJ, England

The map on page vi is reprinted from Zygmunt G. Barański and Rebecca J. West, eds., *The Cambridge Companion to Modern Italian Culture* (Cambridge: Cambridge University Press, 2001). Reprinted with the permission of Cambridge University Press.

The map on page 60 is reprinted from MacGregor Knox, *Hitler's Italian Allies: Royal Armed Forces, Fascist Regime, and the War of 1940–1943* (Cambridge: Cambridge University Press, 2000). Reprinted with the permission of Cambridge University Press.

British Library Cataloguing in Publication Information Available

Library of Congress Cataloging-in-Publication Data

Domenico, Roy Palmer.
    Remaking Italy in the twentieth century / Roy Palmer Domenico.
        p. cm.—(Critical issues in history)
Includes bibliographical references and index.
    ISBN 0-8476-9636-7 (alk. paper)—ISBN 0-8476-9637-5 (pbk. : alk. paper)
    1. Italy—History. I. Title. II. Series.
DG467 .D66 2002
945.091—dc21   2002004541

Printed in the United States of America

♾™ The paper used in this publication meets the minimum requirements of American National Standard for Information Sciences—Permanence of Paper for Printed Library Materials, ANSI/NISO Z39.48-1992.

Contents

SWITZERLAND   formerly   AUSTRIA
               South Tyrol

TRENTINO-
ALTO-
ADIGE
Trent

VALLE
D'AOSTA   Milan   FRIULI-
Aosta   VENEZIA   Caporetto
                              GIULIA
Turin   LOMBARDY   VENETO
           Cremona   Trieste
PIEDMONT   R.Po   Venice ISTRIA Rijeka (Fiume)
                                         (to Italy 1924)
        L I G U R I A
                EMILIA ROMAGNA
           Genoa   Bologna   D
                                            A
                                            L
                      San Marino   M
                                            A
           Florence   T
                          Ancona   I
        TUSCANY   A

                    Perugia   A
CORSICA   UMBRIA   d
(France)   r
                                   i
                    L'Aquila   a
            LAZIO   t
            Rome   ABRUZZI   i
                                   c
                                   S
                    MOLISE   e
                      Campobasso   a
            SARDINIA
                      CAMPANIA   A
                      Naples   P
                                      U
                                      L
                      Potenza   I
                                      A
            Cagliari
                      BASILICATA

        T y r r h e n i a n
            S e a   C
                                     A
                                     L
                                     A
                                     B
                          Catanzaro R
                                     I
                                     A
            Palermo

0   100   200 km   N
0   100 miles

S I C I L Y

Acquisitions by Italy from
treaty settlements 1919-20
Boundary of Italy after 1947
Regional boundaries
Regional capitals

MALTA

Foreword

IN THE NINETEENTH CENTURY, nationalism emerged as a decisive
force that reshaped European boundaries, standardized lan-
guages, transformed politics, and subverted local customs and traditional values. Out of this cauldron of nationalism, the modern
state of Italy emerged. Yet, even as nationalism transformed Italian
politics and society, regionalism and tradition continued to find
expression in Italy, often acting as bulwarks to national unity, cultural integration, and political harmony. Even as late as 1991, as
Roy Domenico observes, only 48 percent of Italians used the national tongue when speaking with friends and colleagues. That
local and regional dialects continued to be spoken in daily conversations suggests that "modernity" did not come easily to Italy.

Indeed, inexorable regionalism and intransigent traditional culture, manifested especially in the Roman Catholic Church, defied
the inevitability of modernity and those features associated with
it—Enlightenment values, industrialization, centralized government, secularization, and, more to the point, the eradication of
pronounced regionalism and entrenched traditionalism. Arguably
one of the most apparent signs of this tension between the past
and, if you will, the future was evident in the struggle between the

tradition of Roman Catholicism, as an institutional, political, and cultural force, and those Enlightenment political philosophies of Liberalism, Marxism, and Fascism. Much of the nineteenth century and early twentieth century in Italy was to be shaped by this political and cultural contest between Roman Catholicism and Liberalism, Marxism, and Fascism. Thus it is not without some irony, Domenico shows, that the dominant Catholic political party, the Christian Democrats, in the post–World War II period, ushered in postmodern culture and society with its associated features of pronounced consumerism, narcissistic individualism, bureaucratic statism, cultural and ethnic diversity, and rejection of traditional values and local custom.

Domenico deftly places the development of modern Italy from the nineteenth century through the contemporary period in a larger political and cultural perspective. In doing so, he crafts a compelling account of political contests among Liberalism, Marxism, Fascism, and Catholicism, while showing how these ideological struggles affected both high and popular culture, including opera, music, architecture, film, and even eating and drinking habits. Along the way, readers are introduced to those fascinating figures that shaped both Italian culture, as well as European and American culture. In *Remaking Italy*, readers are introduced to revolutionaries such as Giuseppe Mazzini and Giuseppe Garibaldi, authors such as Carlo Lorenzetti (*Pinocchio*) and Gabriele D'Annunzio (*The Virgins of the Rocks*), and Marxist theorist Antonio Gramsci and Fascist leader Benito Mussolini. Readers meet the great operatic composer Giuseppe Verdi and the master conductor and musician Arturo Toscanini, the Nobel Prize–winning playwright Luigi Pirandello, and the painter Giorgio De Chirico. So, too, readers encounter those Roman Catholic popes who sought to temper, if not correct, the forces of secularism, liberalism, and capitalism: Pius IX, who wrote the reactionary "Syllabus of Errors"; Leo XIII, who issued the influential encyclical *Rerum novarum*; Pius XI, the author of *Quadrigesimo anno*; and the first Polish pope, Karol Wojtila, who became John Paul II. Readers also learn that while filmmaker Federico Fellini changed movies, media mogul Silvio Berlusconi brought new theater to contemporary Italian politics.

In telling us about those who shaped modern Italy, Domenico reveals how a backward agricultural society—divided by region, language, and culture—was transformed into a modern state, still faced with regional tension, ethnic divisions, and the problems inherent in postmodern society.

Donald T. Critchlow
Series Editor

Acknowledgments

I OWE GREAT DEBTS to many friends and colleagues who contributed advice, ideas, and support as I worked on this manuscript, and I thank them. Any mistakes or errors of judgment contained in the following pages are, of course, entirely my own and were committed in spite of their assistance. Rebecca Brittenham, Jonathan Nashel, Lynn Berrettoni-Caglieris, George Sirgiovanni, Jim Fisher, Kristina Chew, Helen Holmes, Beverly Anderson, Palmer and Barbara Domenico, and Lil and Gene Minogue all gave more than they received. The University of Scranton History Department shouldered too much of my burden, particularly its chair, Michael De Michele, and Frank Homer, Lee Penyak, and Bob Shaffern, who read and commented on chapters. Dozens of students in my "Modern Italy" classes, moreover, provided piercing critiques of this work while it was in progress. I persistently relied on Jodi Dunn and Virginia Picchietti of the Scranton Italian Studies group for quick information fixes. I leaned on Rosemarie Pryle for crucial help in a pinch, and she never disappointed me. Her ever-loyal troops, Ashley Graf, Liz Scoblick, Karen Swikata, and Henry Yampolsky, undertook much of the foot work of copying and collating. Sheila Ferraro and Magdalene Ristuccia of the

Weinberg Memorial Library Interlibrary Loan Desk are the unsung heroes, without whom there would be no book. Don Critchlow, Mary Carpenter, and Erin McKindley at Rowman & Littlefield allowed me more time to finish than I deserved. My wife, Robin, and our children, Katie, Johnny, Matthew, and Clare, provided me with love, patience, and inspiration. Finally, Lamberto Mercuri not only read the manuscript, but he and his wife, Vera, lived much of it, and it is to them that I dedicate this work.

Abbreviations

AC/ACC	Allied Commission/Allied Control Commission
ANICA	Associazione Nazionale Industrie Cinematografiche Audiovisive
BR	Brigate Rosse
CGIL	Confederazione Generale Italiana del Lavoro
CGL	Confederazione Generale del Lavoro
CISL	Confederazione Italiana Sindacati Lavoratori
CL	Comunione e Liberazione
CLN	Comitato di Liberazione Nazionale
CLNAI	Comitato di Liberazione Nazionale Alt'Italia
DC	Democrazia Cristiana
ECSC	European Coal and Steel Community
EIAR	Ente Italiano Audizione Radiofoniche
ENI	Ente Nazionale Idrocarburi
ERP	European Recovery Program
EUR	Esposizione Universale di Roma
FIOM	Federazione Italiana Operai Metallurgici
FUCI	Federazione Universitaria Cattolica Italiana
GAP	Gruppi d'Azione Pattriotica
IMI	Istituto Mobiliare Italiano

IRI	Istituto per la Ricostruzione Industriale
MSI	Movimento Sociale Italiano
MVSN	Milizia Volontaria per la Sicurezza Nazionale
NATO	North Atlantic Treaty Organization
ONMI	Opera Nazionale per la Maternità ed Infanzia
OSS	Office of Strategic Services
PCI	Partito Comunista Italiano
PDS	Partito Democratico della Sinistra
PLI	Partito Liberale Italiano
PNF	Partito Nazionale Fascista
PPI	Partito Popolare Italiano
PR	Partito Radicale
PRI	Partito Repubblicano Italiano
PSDI	Partito Social-Democratico Italiano
PSI	Partito Socialista Italiano
PSLI	Partito Socialista dei Lavoratori Italiani
PSU	Partito Socialista Unitario
RAI	Radio Audizioni Italiane
RSI	Repubblica Sociale Italiana
SAP	Squadre di Azione Patriottica
UDI	Unione di Donne Italiane
UIL	Unione Italiana del Lavoro
UNRRA	United Nations Rehabilitation and Relief Administration
UQ	Uomo Qualunque
URI	Unione Radiofonica Italiana

1

Liberal Apex and Crisis

ITALIANS HAVE LONG BEEN FAMILIAR with an idea attributed, perhaps incorrectly, to Massimo D'Azeglio. Italy, he was supposed to have claimed, had been "made," but the task remained to make Italians. A Piedmontese artist and statesman, D'Azeglio referred here to the Risorgimento, Italy's nineteenth-century struggle for liberation and unity that concluded in September 1870 when soldiers of King Victor Emmanuel II took the city of Rome from Pope Pius IX. The Italian tricolored flag, a recent invention, now fluttered above the Eternal City, the new capital of the new nation of Italy.

The Risorgimento had thus "made Italy" in the sense that it finalized the basic contours of the country's political geography, from a border in the Alps down to Sicily and the Mediterranean Sea, barely one hundred miles from the shores of Africa. The Italians had realized their frontiers, but now they faced a new challenge: to determine the shape of their nation's society and its culture, to forge what Italy was really all about. The Risorgimento and its immediate legacy lasted through the end of the nineteenth century.

By the first decade of the twentieth century, most of the Risorgimento leaders had passed the torch to a younger generation. King

Victor Emmanuel III, for example, was thirty-one years old in 1900 when he took the throne after years of strife that culminated in the assassination of his father, Umberto I. An optimism marked the first years of the young king's reign that complemented the new century. By 1900, many of Italy's kinks seemed to have been worked out. The economic and political tumults of the 1890s had subsided, and the country reached an era of prosperity under the able guidance of Prime Minister Giovanni Giolitti, who had been a young man during the Risorgimento although, significantly, he did not participate in the struggle.

The philosopher Benedetto Croce cautioned against the use of "golden age" to describe early twentieth-century Italy. Still, he observed, "as in the life of the individual there are years when a man reaps the fruit of the pains which he has endured and the experiences which he has gathered and suffered . . . so it is in the life of nations." "Never before," he concluded, "had conditions been so favorable" to the development of Italian Liberalism "as they were now."[1] Croce must have despaired when he wrote those considerations in the mid-1920s, when Benito Mussolini's Fascist regime had begun its own attempt to remake Italy and trample on the Liberal freedoms that were dear to him.

The theme of this volume, remaking Italy in the twentieth century, is not an original one. Nor was the concept of remaking Italians original to D'Azeglio. For centuries, others pondered not only Italy's shape but also its purpose. For some, Italy had been the center of the Roman Empire; for others, part of medieval Christendom. The image of medieval and Renaissance communes and states still loomed large, and many considered Italy not to be a nation at all but rather a collection of countries worth more as their parts than as a whole. The nineteenth-century Risorgimento presented a practical if flawed resolution to these debates. That convulsion, along with the chaos of early modernization, created a singular opportunity to exploit Italy's potential. The country was still young enough to be sent along one of any number of paths. Italy's road through the twentieth century, however, diverted in a number of sharp turns.

Neither Rome nor Italy was made in a day. The birth of the modern nation followed a long gestation that allowed visionaries to reflect on the shape of the finished product. Some pondered the essential geographic question of location: Where is Italy? Today we might wonder how such an issue could have been open to speculation. Italy is mostly a peninsula with some offshore islands. It is surrounded on three sides by water and on the fourth by the Alps, the highest mountains in Western Europe. But the shape of Italy did not remain constant from one historical stage to the next. In ancient times, the Romans excluded what we know as western Piedmont from Italy. The historian Giuliano Procacci also wondered whether all of pre–sixteenth-century Piedmont could be considered as Italian.[2]

Procacci's question has the ring of truth to it when one considers the guide to Italian food published in the 1500s by Bartolomeo Scappi, the chef of Pope Pius V. He broke Italy into three culinary zones: the south, the center, and "Lombardy," which did not include Piedmont. Such cultural indicators often also set Venice apart, as a world removed from the rest of the country. And Renaissance citizens of Florence, Siena, or Milan directed their fiercest passions at their neighbors rather than against invaders from over the Alps. Even during the Risorgimento, the principal architect of unity, Piedmont's Count Camillo Benso di Cavour, maintained a different vision of Italy than that held by some of his compatriots. D'Azeglio, for instance, broke with Cavour when the former questioned the wisdom of uniting the south and the north.

Beyond the frontier issue, geography divides Italy internally as well. The Apennine mountains, for example, drop south into Italy from the Alps and slice the nation in half, right down the middle. Mountainous and rugged terrain constitute a fact of life that has influenced much of Italy's identity. Less than a quarter of Italy is flatlands. Indeed, most of its large cities sit within eyeshot of mountains. The landscape is lovely and often awesome but also daunting; and it aggravates Italy's long thin shape. It is a nation roughly the size of Nevada in land area; but from west to east, only

172 kilometers (about 107 miles) divide Rome near the Tyrrhenian Sea from Pescara on the Adriatic, while, north to south, 1,271 kilometers (about 790 miles) separate Milan from Reggio Calabria.

Italian geographic realities, moreover, promoted a legacy of cultural, economic, and social divisions. The Po valley of Bologna, Pavia, and Alessandria is far removed from Apulia's Tavoliere, while Sardinia's history is closer to Barcelona's than it is to Venice's. Milan and Turin are nearer to Zurich and Paris than they are to Sicily. Such matters have influenced visions of what a country should look like and have accentuated the differences between wealthier European Italy in the north and poorer Mediterranean Italy in the south.

To solve the question of geography was a simple task compared to another challenge, that of purpose. What *kind* of country would Italy be, a controversy that still awaits a satisfactory resolution. Many visions have contested with each other since at least the nineteenth century. The new country in 1870 offered itself as a laboratory for ideas of statecraft and society. Italians tested different formulas but never reached a consensus on the right solution; the student might consider the past century as one of struggles between factions that aimed to seize the moment and fashion their young country according to their own visions.

This survey of twentieth-century Italy will illustrate endeavors undertaken by partisans of competing philosophies—each designed to mold the nation according to its particular vision. Most important among them were Liberals, Catholics, Marxists, and Fascists. The Liberals took their turn first and remade Italy during the period from the national unification to World War I. Next came the Fascists, followed by a Catholic faction, the Christian Democrats. At the turn of the twenty-first century new forces, akin to the old Liberals, have emerged to put their stamp on Italy. For the Marxists, the twentieth century has been a long and frustrating journey that sometimes placed them near the center of power but never yielded them full rein. It was only in 1998, ironically, when an ex-Communist, Massimo D'Alema, assumed the prime minister's chair.

While Liberals, Fascists, and Christian Democrats triumphed in turn, and even achieved something that approached hegemony, no faction ever ruled entirely by itself or without challenge. Even the Fascist dictatorship was tempered, sometimes even publicly confronted, by rivals in the Catholic Church, in the Royal House, and in the business world. Banished political foes, moreover, continued to operate underground in preparation for actions to come.

Each political faction was further distinguished by its own internal dissent and myriad subgroups. The Marxist camp, for example, has been home to communists and socialists, partisans of Antonio Gramsci, Joseph Stalin, and Mao Zedong, or those gathered in alternative factions such as Lotta Continua or the Red Brigades. Later other groups, independent of the Marxists, such as feminists and environmentalists, emerged to join or replace the older ones and contest the status quo.

The Risorgimento Background

Italians chose the term *Risorgimento* to represent their liberation and unification. It was a term first used in the eighteenth century by the poet Vittorio Alfieri, the Piedmontese aristocrat who closely followed the Revolutionary War in America and dedicated verse to George Washington. Alfieri employed *Risorgimento* to conjure the image of a long-dormant fountain. In the nineteenth century the fountain's dancing sprays would open up again and be allowed to "resurge," or *risorgere*. The idea grew and found support, particularly among the nascent liberals, northern merchant classes, and romantics. The Risorgimento was without question a great drama: the liberation and union of a people, and the establishment of a free nation.

The age of the Risorgimento began in 1796 when France invaded Italy. From Turin to Naples, victorious troops of the Franco-Italian warrior Napoleon Bonaparte spread the inflammatory pitch of the French Revolution. They brought the principles of bourgeois republic to groups as disparate as Milanese businessmen, many of whom eagerly accepted them, and Apulian peasants, many of whom did not. Before the royal and ducal courts of Turin, Florence, and Naples, the French ushered the specter of regicide. To the ancient lands of Italy—the Republic of Venice, the States of the Church, the Grand Duchy of Tuscany, the Kingdoms of Naples and Sardinia—Napoleon resurrected the ideal of the united nation.

Napoleon redesigned Italy twice after two very different conquests. He undertook his first invasion of 1796 as a revolutionary, forging the country mainly into four republics: the Cisalpine, anchored by the Po River with its capital at Milan; the Ligurian, around Genoa; the Roman in central Italy; and the Parthenopean (Naples) in the south. By 1799, however, France lost the gains of its first conquest to the fortunes of war, and, the following year, Napoleon launched a second invasion. His second try, eventually as an emperor, cast Italy not into republics but kingdoms. The Kingdom of Italy stretched from Milan down the east coast to Ancona, while the Kingdom of Naples occupied the south, except for Sicily and Sardinia, which enjoyed British protection. Most of the rest, including Rome, was eventually absorbed into France.

Napoleon's empire crumbled in 1813, and, after his trusted brother-in-law and representative Gioacchino Murat died, Italy reverted back to what Prince Metternich of Austria dismissed as a "geographical expression." The victors' Congress of Vienna redrew the map and recognized Piedmont as an independent state in the northwest that controlled the remote island of Sardinia and awarded it the old Genoese Republic along the Ligurian coast. Next, Lombardy and Venetia in the north and northeast were linked as a puppet kingdom under an Austrian viceroy. Vienna also indirectly controlled satellite duchies and principalities in what are today Tuscany and part of Emilia-Romagna, while the resurrected Papal States stretched again across the peninsula from Rome to Ancona. Southern Italy and Sicily formed the Kingdom of the Two Sicilies under Bourbon monarchs who returned to Naples from their British haven in Palermo.

The idea of unification, however, remained strong. Revolutions in 1820–21 and 1831 against Austrian domination and reactionary regimes may have met with defeat, but Italy's journey on the road toward liberation gathered steam. More of a sense of purpose came from influential thinkers such as Vincenzo Gioberti, whose "Guelph" vision appealed for a united nation under a papal presidency, or Giuseppe Mazzini, with his calls for a holy and inspired democracy. In 1848–49 much of the peninsula briefly joined in the disastrous "First War of the Risorgimento" against Austria. The Italian states, however, found that they could not go it alone against Vienna's army, which twice crushed the forces of King Carlo Alberto of Piedmont. Humiliated, he abdicated the throne and died shortly thereafter.

Italy had to wait another decade before victory and unification. A new generation rose under Carlo Alberto's son and successor, Piedmont's new king Victor Emmanuel II, and under Prime Minister Cavour. Count Cavour was a nobleman who spoke less Italian than French and displayed little interest in the south. But he was also a political mastermind who embarked on a brilliant mission to expand and consolidate the power of his king. The catastrophe of 1848–49 made him realize that help from a foreign power was necessary to oppose Austria, and consequently he turned to France. But for Paris's support in a war of national unification, Emperor Louis Napoleon demanded the high price of two Piedmontese territories: Savoy, the homeland of the royal family, and Nice, the birthplace of the hero of unification, Giuseppe Garibaldi.

French support provided the necessary push for the initial success of the conflict that followed, the Second War of the Risorgimento. In 1859, a Franco-Piedmontese army took Lombardy from Austria, and the central duchies quickly joined the new union. But what of the south? The Bourbon kingdom remained outside the scope of most northern nationalists. Garibaldi, however, forced the issue in May 1860 by landing a ragtag volunteer army of his own in Sicily and marching up the peninsula to Naples. Distinguished by their red shirts, his renegade troops

brought down the Kingdom of the Two Sicilies and ushered its
union with Piedmont.

Flushed with success, Garibaldi continued north toward Rome
where, during the revolutionary days of eleven years before, he
and Mazzini had led a brief and unsuccessful republic. But since
1849, the Holy See enjoyed the protection of French troops, and
an attack on Rome would have forced an embarrassing international incident. The apprehensive Cavour acted quickly to head
off Garibaldi by invading from the north and annexing the eastern Papal States without entering Rome.

The next step toward complete unification occurred in 1866
when Italy supported Prussia in the Seven Weeks War against Austria. Its performance in the conflict was at best minimal, although
the goal of annexing Venetia was achieved at the peace table. Italian unification was largely completed by the addition of Rome in
1870. The outbreak of the Franco-Prussian War that year forced
Louis Napoleon to withdraw his troops from the city and leave the
pope defenseless. Victor Emmanuel promptly seized the opportunity to invade the ancient city on September 20, 1870, and make
it his capital.

The framers of the new Italy were the victors of the Risorgimento. Their leaders were, first, Cavour, who died in 1861, then
others such as D'Azeglio, Agostino Depretis, and Francesco
Crispi. To portray all of them as Liberals is to stretch that term to
its widest and most unwieldy nineteenth-century definition. Post-
Risorgimento Italian Liberalism was sloppy and flawed, charac-
terized by an unhealthy reliance on the state among industrialists
and nationalists; chained by landholders, the monarchy, and the
aristocracy; and at war with the Catholic Church.

Still, the Liberals enjoyed a certain cohesion. While they
fought in parliament over nuances of free trade and imperialism, not much really distinguished one from the other. Ideolo-
gies and parties did not divide Italy's Chamber of Deputies and
Senate so much as did personalities or interest groups. Most leg-
islators agreed on some form of private enterprise, on capitalism, and on civil liberties when they did not get out of hand.

Most accepted the monarchy, albeit sometimes grudgingly. They were generally and loosely nationalists, and they thrived in the clubby world of nineteenth century legislatures. Eloquence and facile oratorical grasps of Cicero and Dante were badges they proudly wore. But the big-tent nature of Italian parliamentary politics, personified in the 1870s and 1880s by Prime Minister Depretis, a conniving master of patron–client relations, alienated outsiders and mavericks such as Andrea Costa, Giustino Fortunato, and Gaetano Salvemini who envisioned other, structured solutions to Italian problems. As time went on these critics multiplied and formed political organizations that interfered with Rome's more established and ideologically bland arrangement. But until World War I, the men of the Risorgimento and their progeny kept hold of the reins.

Economic and Social Challenges

Notwithstanding some setbacks in the 1880s and 1890s, by the turn of the century the Italian state had stabilized and the nation's economy had reached what can be termed its "takeoff" period of sustained growth. Agriculture still dominated Italy's economy and would continue to do so well into the twentieth century. Industry, however, had become a significant and growing element. Although coal and steel production could not compare with that of other European powers, it was respectable, and Italy competed with verve in other "new" industries such as metallurgy, hydroelectric power, petrochemicals, and automobiles. Trade figures illustrate some of the picture. Between 1896 and 1900, Italy's exports totaled, on the average, 1.2 billion lire per year. Between 1911 and 1915, the figure reached 1.9 billion. Agriculture's share of the expansion remained more or less constant, from 28.0 percent to 28.9. As a portion of the whole, raw materials declined from 17.2 to 13.4 percent in the same period. Industrial goods, however, filled the gap, from 54.8 to 57.7 percent, and industrial exports more than doubled from 670 million lire to 1.37 billion lire. Yet all figures rose like a row boat on flood waters. Exports of raw materials, for example, increased from 211.2 million lire to 317.5 million.

Rome's reliance on heavy agricultural taxes, the lack of raw resources, the poverty and backwardness of large expanses, particularly in the south, the abuse of workers, and other issues have called into question the extent and authenticity of Italy's turn-of-the-century industrial revolution. One of Italy's most pressing conundrums and ultimately one of its greatest failures was that of widespread poverty. The problem existed everywhere with wretched pockets of want in the north, in Alpine areas, and across the Veneto. But the challenge was particularly vexing in the south, a gnawing pain that runs through the history of modern Italy.

Before the Risorgimento, romantic northerners and foreigners liked to recall ancient Roman descriptions of the south, the Mezzogiorno, as the imperial granary, the "horn of plenty" (*conca d'oro*), and they dreamed of it still as a garden of dormant wealth that begged cultivation by smart liberals and capitalists. Unfortunately, the dream would never be realized; and soon after the Risorgimento, many northerners changed their opinions of the south from a land of opportunity to a place to be tapped and exploited, a corrupt land where superstitious and backward peasants mingled with kidnappers and bandits. Social indicators reflected the disparities between southern poverty and northern prosperity. In 1901, for instance, about 10 percent of the Milanesi were illiterate, while the figure stood at 43 percent in Naples and 60 percent in Benevento.

Dismissed as of little consequence, southern industry languished in neglect and suffered at the hands of northern competition, free trade, and the diversion to the north of government funds from the sale of church lands. Consequently, more industrial jobs existed in Naples in 1871 than in 1911. Competition, furthermore, destroyed the south's silk industry. Rome's remedies for southern misery came only in spotty doses such as earthquake relief in 1908, railroad construction, or port developments in Naples and Taranto.

The Mezzogiorno's agriculture fared no better than did its industry. Government expenditures for land reclamation, for instance, were grossly maldistributed. Between 1867 and 1897, Rome spent 267 million lire on such projects in the north, 188 million on those in the center, while the south received only 3 million. In 1869, furthermore, the state inaugurated its *macinato* tax on the grinding of grain that severely cut into the economy of the overwhelmingly agricultural south. In Sardinia, for example, taxes doubled between 1850 and 1870. It should be said that certain, more advanced agricultural areas, mainly zones in Campania, Apulia, and Sicily, prospered under Italian rule; but most did not, leading to predictable social and political results. As poverty worsened and banditry and crime flourished, Sicily exploded in revolt at the end of the nineteenth century—the Fasci Siciliani rebellion—and southerners began en masse to leave the country altogether. Every year from 1900 to 1914, on average, 616,000 Italians, mostly southerners, bid *addio* to Italy for greener pastures in other lands.

The north's economy fared better. It was closer than was the south to European markets and investors, a particular blessing for banks and railroads. The north benefited from reliable fast-running rivers for mills and, later, for electricity: Europe's first power station opened in Milan in 1883. The north's agricultural traditions were generally more progressive. The north possessed a strong artisan heritage, and, after the Risorgimento, the government favored northern business. Rome felt, for instance, that Italy's expanding railways should purchase fewer foreign locomotives and directed them toward the new Italian companies, Tosi and Breda, both founded in the 1880s.

An important consequence of industrial progress was the growth of a proletariat and of working-class politics. The 1901 census revealed that industry accounted for 23.8 percent of the nation's workforce, a large and growing faction with potential for real change. The working class began to mobilize and organize often with a Marxist or left-wing outlook. An early manifestation was the Left's radical Democracy League, founded in 1879 by the aged firebrand Garibaldi. The expansion of the franchise also put more and more men on the voting rolls, new voices heard in greater numbers, and in 1883, Andrea Costa became the first socialist elected to the Chamber of Deputies, a victory that was a sign of things to come.

More than any other, the Socialist Party became the standard bearer of the working class. It organized at a Genoa Congress in 1892 under the leadership of Filippo Turati and Anna Kuliscioff. Born in 1857, Turati began as a lawyer and a writer who identified with the Italian Workers Party (Partito Operaio Italiano), a forerunner of the Socialists that enjoyed a brief life in the 1880s. Turati became both intellectually and romantically attached to Kuliscioff, a Russian émigré who had broken a romance with Andrea Costa. As partners at the helm, Turati and Kuliscioff steered the party along a moderate, "minimalist" course in the 1890s and into the first decade of the twentieth century. Under Turati and Kuliscioff, however, in 1901 the Socialists came out in support of the moderate Luigi Zanardelli ministry and came increasingly to be identified as allies of the Giolitti wing of Liberalism.

Government reaction to worker's discontent, however, was not always distinguished by restraint. Rome sometimes met the challenge with ruthless violence, particularly in Milan's Fatti di Maggio riots of 1898 where General Fiorenzo Bava Beccaris fired cannons directly into a rioting crowd. For this, the general received a decoration from King Umberto who had come to the throne in 1878 after the death of his father, Victor Emmanuel II. An anarchist, in turn, killed Umberto in 1900 while he attended a gymnastics meet at Monza. Victor Emmanuel III followed his father and would reign until 1946.

Through the first apprehensive decades of worker organization, Socialists debated their own tactics and aims. In 1904, a radical, "Maximalist" faction pushed the moderates aside and ambitiously proclaimed Italy's first "general strike." The strike failed, however, and discredited the Maximalists. Then more seriously in 1912, the hard-liners assumed command of the party, the result of the debate over Italy's colonial war against the Ottoman Empire. Despite all the squabbles, however, the party continued to grow, climbing from a handful of deputies at the turn of the century to become the parliament's largest single faction by World War I. Numbers can be deceiving, however, in that the Liberals herded in factions more than they did in parties, as such, and, taken as a whole, they still vastly outnumbered the Socialists.

The Catholic Church provided another challenge for Italy's Liberal governments. During the Risorgimento, Giovanni Maria Mastai Ferretti led the church. A cleric from the northeast Marche region, he took the name Pius IX upon his election to the Throne of St. Peter in 1846. Some observers were initially encouraged by what they saw as progressive strains in his character. But 1848 placed Pope Pius IX squarely against unification. In November, a revolutionary atmosphere prompted him to disguise himself and flee to Gaeta on the coast where the king of Naples could protect him. In the Eternal City, the republican radical Giuseppe Garibaldi helped to establish a republic in February 1849, and Mazzini arrived shortly after to participate in a ruling triumvirate. The brief Roman revolution crashed in flames, and the pontiff returned with the help of Spanish, Neapolitan, and French troops.

Still, the idea of national unity lived on, now more and more coupled with secularist Liberalism. At the forefront of the unification movement, Piedmont confronted Pius with other headaches such as the 1850 Siccardi Laws, which abrogated many church privileges and allowed for civil marriage. Struggle over compliance with this legislation, furthermore, resulted in the incarceration and exile of Turin's archbishop. Things were made worse in 1859 when the Casati Laws launched the laicization of the school system and attempted to pull education from the church's grip, measures that Piedmont extended to the larger kingdom after the unification.

In 1860, when it seemed that relations could not sink any lower, Cavour aggravated tensions by invading the Papal States. Piedmont's aggression was designed to stop Garibaldi and his Red Shirt followers from taking Rome as the last link in uniting north and south. But French troops, since 1849, remained garrisoned in the city and committed to the defense of Pius IX. The prospect of Garibaldi igniting an international incident sent the Piedmontese into a panic. Therefore, to neutralize Garibaldi's march on Rome from the south, troops of King Victor Emmanuel II violated the pope's domains from the north; and at Castelfidardo on September 18, they fired on Pius's outnumbered forces. On October 26, the king and his troops reached Garibaldi at Teano, and the Red Shirts dutifully disbanded. There, Victor Emmanuel extended his hand to the hero of Italian unification despite snubs from the arrogant and second-rate Piedmontese generals, who considered him an unworthy plebeian.

A consequence of the monarch's end run at Teano was the absorption of the eastern Papal States into his new kingdom. Rome, however, remained in papal hands and friction persisted between united Italy and the pope. In 1862, the new government took control of many Catholic charity organizations and in 1867 confiscated and sold off a number of monasteries. The Holy See retaliated with the *Non expedit,* which evolved in the 1860s and ordered the faithful to boycott national elections. For a country of Catholics, the consequences were dire.

The final rupture between church and state occurred in 1870 when the Franco-Prussian War required France to recall its Roman garrison, leaving the city and the pope vulnerable to attack. Italy promptly seized the opportunity. Victor Emmanuel's cannons blew a hole in the Roman walls near Michelangelo's Porta Pia, a breach wide enough to allow the royal army to enter the city with ease and proclaim it the capital of Italy. Pius retreated into the Vatican and proclaimed that it would be his prison. He excommunicated everyone responsible for the invasion and cut formal ties to the Italian state. In response, the new Roman government adopted a hands-off policy toward the pontiff and later offered him a generous compensation package, the 1871 "Law of Papal Guarantees." This measure gave the pope absolute freedom of action, protected him from assassinations and insults, and provided funds equal to the old Papal State budget for the administration of his affairs. But the Liberals argued at cross purposes with Pius IX. Compensation did not interest him, and he never took the money. Rather, he yearned for the return of the ancient patrimony of St. Peter that had been stolen from him and the Universal Church in the name of nationhood and progress. This "Roman Question" remained the painful thorn in church–state relations until well into the twentieth century. It meant the Italian government could not rely on the support of "good" Catholics. It also made things easier for anticlerical "priest eaters" in the Parliament to engage in measures such as the conscription of clergy, the prohibition of church activity in politics, and the various endeavors of Prime Minister Francesco Crispi, who excelled in both major offenses and petty irritants. His legislation in 1890 squeezed the clergy out of much of the remaining charity and welfare societies and replaced them with state bureaucrats. A year before in Rome's Campo dei Fiori, Crispi tweaked the Vatican's nose by dedicating a statue of Giordano Bruno on the spot where the heretical monk had been burned at the stake in 1600.

Pius IX died in 1878—the end of a thirty-two-year-reign that was the longest in the church's history. The contentious old man's corpse, however, suffered a final indignity three years later when the Holy See transferred it across town from the Vatican to the basilica of San Lorenzo. To avoid trouble, the cortege snuck out of the Vatican in the middle of the night, but it was still attacked by a gang of Liberals who tried to throw the coffin into the Tiber. The police intervened just in time to save the pope from a watery grave. Pius's successor, Gioacchino Pecci, the cardinal bishop of Perugia, was elected to the throne of St. Peter on February 20, 1878. Born near Frosinone to a family of the lesser nobility, Pecci chose the pontifical name Leo XIII. Like Pius, Leo enjoyed a long reign until his death in 1903. He explored different angles from which to deal with modern secular states and, in particular, with Italy, but the Roman Question would remain unsolved. Determined to avoid international isolation, Leo immediately worked to repair relations with France and patch them with Germany. His endeavors bore fruit in Germany but not in France after the fall of

Marshal Marie MacMahon's conservative monarchist government. The early 1890s ushered a brief time of goodwill between
the Holy See and Paris although the decade ended in the catastrophe of the Dreyfus affair and the collapse of hopes for better relations.

While reconciliation between the Holy See and the government proved elusive, Italian Catholics undertook different paths
toward working with the new state. Like those on the political
left, Catholics began to mobilize. They did so in two ways. The
first concerned what became known as Catholic Action, the
Azione Cattolica, an enormous lay association. A second route,
particularly in the north, took the form of very successful coop-
eratives and mutual aid societies, often grassroots activity just
short of political organization. The greatest of these enterprises
took the name Opere dei Congressi. Led by the renegade priest,
Romolo Murri, it enjoyed the goodwill of the pontiff, whose
1891 encyclical *Rerum novarum* defended the workers against
the capitalist threat to turn them into commodities or mere cogs
in the big machine. While the document warned that atheistic
socialism was no solution to the problems of the proletariat, Leo
sympathized with the workers' search for dignity and a better
life. Consequently, he harkened back to the medieval tradition of
Catholic corporatism as a way to bring together labor and management on an equal footing. *Rerum novarum*'s message was
taken up by such leading Catholic activists as Giuseppe Toniolo,
an economist at the University of Pisa; by Filippo Meda, editor
of the influential *Catholic Observer* (*L'osservatore cattolico*); and
by the future leader of political Catholicism, the Sicilian priest
Don Luigi Sturzo.

Papal support of the Opere did not continue under Leo's
skeptical successor. Elected in 1903, the next pope was Giuseppe
Sarto, a holy man of humble Veneto roots more concerned with
pastoralism than politics. An indication of Sarto's direction was
his choice of pontifical name, Pius X, to honor Leo's predecessor, the intransigent Mastai Ferretti. The prospect of Murri and
the Opere running away beyond his control disturbed Pius, and

he disbanded the organization in 1904, channeling lay activism into the more pliant Catholic Action. The rebellious Murri was relieved of his priestly duties in 1907 and excommunicated in 1909. He later supported Fascism but was accepted back into the church before his death in 1944. Still, Pius's attack did not defuse Catholic political activity. Regardless of his aims, the faithful were slowly but surely entering the arena. Luigi Sturzo's own experience serves as an illustration. Already elected to the city council of his native Caltagirone in 1899, he became its mayor in 1905.

Cultural Questions

In the newly united country, culture assumed a vital role in the debate over Italian identity, over how the people should think and act as members of a nation. This meant that ancient regional cultures should step aside for a lofty new civic one modeled in Rome and in Florence, Italy's cultural capital.

Dialect traditions of song, theater, and storytelling had to make way for the standard Italian language, modeled on its Tuscan variant, the "language of Dante." This was a formidable challenge since only about 650,000 people out of 25,000,000 spoke "Dante's" Italian in 1860. The new national language was ordered spoken in military ranks and in schools and coerced in public spaces such as government offices, banks, and stores. Still, results were spotty. Italian succeeded most in big cities and bourgeois circles, but it barely affected the peasant class, a situation that would not change until the advent of radio and then, even more so, with television. Still, polling results revealed that as late as 1991, only 48 percent of Italians used the national tongue when speaking with friends and colleagues.

The new language carried with it a new mentality. Books for children, in particular, best conveyed the image that Italy's liberal builders wished to spread. The message of Edmondo De Amicis's work might be compared to those found in America's Horatio

Alger tales or the stories told by Britain's Samuel Smiles. De Amicis's most popular novel, *Cuore* (*Heart: A Schoolboy's Journal*, 1886), exalted themes of duty, hard work, and good citizenship. The same can be found in the internationally acclaimed writings of Carlo Lorenzetti, known in print as Carlo Collodi. His *Le avventure di Pinocchio* (*The Adventures of Pinocchio*, 1883) counseled youngsters to discard the reckless life embodied in the puppet and replace it with the responsible and sober ways of the proper young man.

Regarding the written word, Gabriele d'Annunzio straddled the worlds of highbrow art and popular culture. Born in Pescara in 1863, d'Annunzio was an avant-garde poet and playwright who shocked yet attracted bourgeois audiences with nationalist and Nietzschean themes in such works as *Le vergini delle rocce* (*The Virgins of the Rocks*, 1895). But he was also a true celebrity in an era when few if any Italians could claim that. d'Annunzio, who lost an eye in a duel, lived up to a scandalous reputation in his dalliances with artists and the high born, including a long affair with the acclaimed actress, Eleanora Duse. His mass appeal was no doubt enhanced when he dabbled in celluloid, as a title writer for Giovanni Pastrone's groundbreaking film of 1914, *Cabiria*.

The nascent film industry brought some prestige to Italy and quickly became a major source of innovations. One of Italy's first structures built for the purpose of showing films was Rome's "Moderno," which opened in 1901. The industry was chaotic and, as David Forgacs has noted, "precarious." But it was also creative and internationally popular. By 1912, Italy had become a net exporter of films, a situation that, on the verge of the Great War, it would not enjoy for long.

Italy's high culture, on the other hand, although uneven, generally retained its international prestige. Italian ballet witnessed a renaissance, but the symphony never took firm hold. The late nineteenth-century *macchiaoli* school of painters maintained a respectable but backseat position compared to the French painters although Italy's Futurist movement brought the nation back to center stage in the early twentieth. Some of its major exponents lived in Paris, but the paintings and sculpted works of Umberto Boccioni, Carlo Carrà, Gino Severini, and others refocused the attention of the international art set on Italy before World War I. Italy also continued in its roles as teacher and classroom for aspiring artists around the world.

Italy's premier artist from the unification until his death in 1901, however, was neither a painter nor a sculptor but a composer, Giuseppe Verdi. No other works are more closely linked to the unification movement than are his operas. Born to a family of innkeepers near Parma in 1813, his masterpieces such as *La Traviata* and *Rigoletto* secured for him a global following. But from the 1840s until the 1860s, he also served the nationalist cause in his works such as *The Battle of Legnano*, *Attila*, and *Nabucco*, a tale of the Jewish bondage in Babylon from which the beloved chorus, "Va pensiero," has become Italy's unofficial national anthem.

The end of that most prolific period coincided with the resolution of the Risorgimento; but Verdi's later mature phase was distinguished by even greater triumphs: The *Requiem*, which he dedicated to the nationalist writer Alessandro Manzoni, and his last three operas, *Aida* (1871), *Otello* (1887), and *Falstaff* (1893). In 1901, the aged Verdi took ill in Milan and spent his final days in bed near the La Scala Opera Theater. Completely aware that the end had come for one of Italy's national treasures, the mayor ordered the street facing Verdi's rooms covered with hay to muffle the noise.

Colonial Adventure

Cultural issues, along with struggles among Liberals, Socialists, and Catholics, paralleled Italy's foreign problems. Eric Hobsbawm has described the turn of the century as Europe's "age of empire." Not to be left behind, the government in Rome joined the other imperialist powers and put the nation on a course of colonial expansion. Italy made its imperial choice early. By 1869, its flag flew over Assab, a village on Africa's Red Sea coast, even before it flew over Rome. The decision to search abroad for empire was never entirely popular, and opponents questioned it from many angles: the morality of a newly freed nation attacking weaker peoples, the Risorgimento's unfinished business with Austria that demanded priority over adventure in exotic places, the cost of such operations, and the risk. By looking for colonies, the Italians placed themselves in dangerous competition with Britain, France, Germany, and other countries.

Still, empire had its advocates. Before the turn of the century, their champion was Francesco Saverio Crispi, superpatriot and prime minister in the 1880s and 1890s. He and his nationalist followers regarded colonial expansion as a requisite for great power status. Others felt that the hemorrhage of immigrants to other nations might be better channeled into Italian colonies. Proselytism enticed many Catholics although the church condemned holy war. The Dante Alighieri Society, the Italian Geographic Society (the Royal Italian Geographic Society after 1913), and the Italian National Association (Associazione Nazionale Italiana), founded in 1910 by Enrico Corradini, joined the chorus of pressure groups for colonial expansion. The aristocratic and staid first two, however, were eclipsed by the energy and the radical aims of the last one. At its first national congress in Florence, Corradini declared that "just as socialism taught the proletariat the value of the class struggle, we must teach Italy the value of international struggle. You ask, but the international struggle implies war? Well, let it be war!"[3] Such provocations would often embarrass Italy.

Africa was the target of Italy's imperialist ambitions with most hopes pinned on two parts of the continent, the northern littoral closest to Italy, and the "horn" on the east coast from Eritrea to Somalia. In the Mediterranean, less than one hundred miles from Sicily sat Tunisia, where Dido had loved and cursed Aeneas and the land where once dwelt ancient Rome's mortal enemies, the Carthaginians. It was the obvious goal for many

Italians who matter-of-factly considered it a satellite. Tens of thousands of immigrants had already planted roots there before Rome encouraged thousands more to emigrate in the 1870s and launched an energetic economic penetration. But Rome lagged behind developments elsewhere. France was also interested in Tunisia and, in 1881, grabbed it before the Italians could. Italy had begun to pay the price for competition with the great powers.

In the east African "Horn," Rome extended its holdings along the Red Sea coast from Assab until the Crispi government created the colony of Eritrea in 1890. On Africa's Indian Ocean coast, Rome pieced together possessions and consolidated them in 1905 as another territory, Somalia. Desert scrub covered most of the two territories, and neither proved lucrative. Italy held them probably because no other nation was interested. Nor were many Italians. By 1913, for example, most of them who lived in Eritrea were government and military personnel. Only sixty-one civilians had chosen to sink roots there.

Independent and land-locked Abyssinia, however, linked Italy's coastal deserts. It was a land of great economic potential with a highland climate more agreeable to Europeans, and Italian imperialists felt that they possessed a special claim to it. The two nations negotiated a semiprotectorate agreement, the Treaty of Ucciali, in 1889.

By 1894, however, the Africans made it clear that they wanted out of the document's constricting terms, and, just as bad for the Italians, the French started to build a railroad from their own Red Sea possession, Djibouti, inland to the Abyssinian capital of Addis Ababa. In Rome, Prime Minister Crispi vowed to intervene before Paris turned east Africa into another Tunisia, and in January 1895 the Italians crossed the border from Eritrea to occupy Tigrè. The Abyssinians launched a counteroffensive and, on March 1, 1896, trapped and defeated General Oreste Baratieri's Italian force at Adowa. The catastrophe devastated nationalists, ended the career of the humiliated Crispi, and put on hold Rome's ambitions in the Horn of Africa. Mussolini later claimed that as a young schoolboy news of Adowa caused him to sob in shame. It was a disgrace he vowed to avenge.

After Adowa, the Italians chose another target closer to home: Libya. Since the sixteenth century, it had been ruled by the Turkish Ottoman Empire as two separate districts, Tripolitania and Cyrenaica. By the first years of the twentieth century, the Italians had established in Libya some, if hardly substantial, interests. Their principal economic presence there was the Bank of Rome, an institution with strong ties to Rome's reactionary "black" aristocracy gathered around the Vatican. Fraternal bonds also united the head of the bank, Romolo Tittoni, and his brother, Tomasso, who served as Italy's foreign minister from 1903 until 1905 and again from 1906 to 1909. Economic calls for empire, such as they were, were joined by a political chorus assembled around a new generation of nationalist orators such as Enrico Corradini and Luigi Federzoni. To capture or undercut this sentiment, the reluctant imperialist Giovanni Giolitti promoted an invasion of the Turkish colony.

On September 29, 1911, therefore, Italy declared war on the Ottoman Empire. Between October 4 and 11, the city of Tripoli was taken, and most of the other coastal towns fell by the end of the month. Rome soon learned, though, that the native population did not welcome the invaders as liberators from the Turkish yoke and a stubborn resistance surfaced. In April and May 1912, after months of fighting in north Africa, the Italian navy took the fight to the Turks by bombing the Dardanelles and effecting landings in the Dodecanese Islands in the Aegean Sea. These events and others, such as a shelling of Beirut and seizures of three French ships suspected of running contraband, brought international pressure on Italy to end the war. That Turkey's Balkan territories hovered on the verge of revolt added to Constantinople's desire to discuss peace. Consequently, in the summer of 1912, both sides came to the table in Switzerland and signed a peace treaty at Lausanne on October 18. Italy had achieved its goal of annexing Libya and had taken the Dodecanese in the bargain. At the cost of 3,500 Italian lives, Rome now possessed a Mediterranean empire.

Foreign Affairs and War

Had Italy now made it into the ranks of the great powers? With a European population roughly equal to France's or Britain's, a robust economy larger than Russia's, and an African empire of sorts, nationalists asked, Why should Italy be excluded? And what Italy lacked in the conventional measurements of great power status—natural resources, for instance, or battlefield glory—it compensated for in the arts, one area that bestowed upon Rome a place in the first rank of nations. But the nagging doubt remained. If the great power club opened its doors to Rome, many feared, the invitation to enter was made with some reluctance.

After the Risorgimento, Italy entered into an alliance with Germany. Rome and Berlin had already joined forces against Austria in 1866; later, Germany's chancellor Otto von Bismarck valued Italy as part of his plan to isolate Paris after the Franco-Prussian War of 1870. In this scheme, rivalry over Tunisia worked to alienate Rome from its Latin cousin, Paris. When France annexed Tunisia, therefore, a startled and enraged Italian state turned to Germany, which, as its price for support, insisted that Rome work toward better relations with its old nemesis, Vienna. A year later, in 1882, Rome, Berlin, and Vienna joined together in the Triple Alliance or "Triplice." German influence in Italy was subsequently cemented through the infusion of capital and the establishment of banks. The Banca Commerciale Italiana was the most famous example, founded in 1894 with German and Austrian resources. But it was not the only one. The Credito Italiano (1895) and the Società Bancaria Italiana (1905) were also established with strong introductions of such funds.

Still, Rome seemed wedded to Berlin and Vienna only until something better came along. Questions over the Triple Alliance arose from the nagging doubt that Italy had more "natural" places to look for friends. The problem lay with Austria. Regardless of the treaty, many, probably most, patriotic Italians still considered the Hapsburg Empire as their enemy, not only because it had played a historic role as master of Venetia and Lombardy but also because, in 1882, it still oppressed captive Italian populations in the northeast zones around Trent and Trieste, territories that, since the Risorgimento, had become known as "unredeemed" Italy (*Italia irredenta*). Furthermore, Vienna was the principal power behind the Holy See, Liberal Italy's alter ego, an unforgivable offense.

Consequently, Italy immediately launched a search for exits from the Triple Alliance and for ties to other nations. In 1887, Rome signed a Mediterranean Agreement with a sympathetic London government under Lord Salisbury. His predecessor, William Gladstone, was an old friend of Liberal Italy who, as a young diplomat, had damned Naples's Bourbon monarchy as a "negation of God." Healthy trade links and colonial cooperation in Africa further strengthened Italy's ties to Britain.

It took longer for relations with France to improve. Bitter memories of Tunisia lingered, problems of Italian immigration to France surfaced, and the two nations waged a disastrous tariff war in the 1880s and 1890s. Nor did Francesco Crispi's Francophobe bluster help. On the other hand, Rome and Paris frequently shared Liberal and anticlerical sentiments; and cultural bonds between the two as Latin "sisters" eventually fostered understanding and better relations. In 1902, Rome and Paris reached the Barrere-Prinetti Accord, an agreement for one to remain neutral if the other was attacked. Both nations, furthermore, supported each other's claims in north Africa, France's on Morocco and Italy's on Libya.

Italy's maneuvers were successful. At the threshold of world war, Italy enjoyed more diplomatic options than did any other European power. In 1914, when Europe's guns of August opened up, Italy's remained silent. Though still tied to the Triplice on paper, Rome rejected intervention and proclaimed its neutrality. Prime Minister Antonio Salandra correctly argued that Italy was not obligated to help Austria since the Hapsburgs had started the conflict as an aggression against Serbia. The alliance had been voided, furthermore, when Vienna reneged on its contractual duty to consult Italy regarding its aims in the Balkans.

Italy's unsettled domestic situation, furthermore, made it reluctant to act in the summer of 1914. Between June 7 and 14, an aborted revolution, the so-called Red Week, paralyzed the city of Ancona and much of nearby Romagna. It began as a largely spontaneous protest against the disciplining of two reluctant soldiers who were to leave for duty in Albania. With little planning or guidance from labor or Socialist leaders, the discontent spread quickly but withered just as fast. Red Week, nevertheless, alarmed the government of the nationalist Salandra, who labeled it a "criminal conspiracy."

Sentiment for peace, furthermore, was quite widespread. It extended across the country and was recognized by a prefectural survey conducted in April 1915. The Prefect of Teramo, for instance, reported that the locals "perceiv[ed] war simply as a disaster, like drought, famine, and the plague." Broad antiwar sentiment was also found in Parliament, where Giolitti counted on a large faction, perhaps even a majority, against intervention. He was joined by most of the Socialist deputies who condemned the war on principles of international workers' solidarity. At the Vatican, too, the new aristocratic pope from Genoa, Benedict XV, opposed the war and would call for an end to its "appalling butchery" and "senseless slaughter." Superpatriots dismissed the Holy See as a nest of traitors and defeatists where the insidious influence of Vienna pervaded. They remembered the election of Pius X in 1903, which had been made possible only when the Austrians vetoed the more Leonine and conciliatory Cardinal Serafino Vannutelli. Nationalist suspicions were reinforced, moreover, by the papacy's continued animus toward Liberal Rome and Paris and its mistrust of France's ally, Orthodox Russia.

That King Victor Emmanuel III's forces were unprepared for such a conflict also dampened calls for war in 1914. Italy, for example, possessed only three hundred machine guns and had no hand grenades or any barbed wire cutters. The Libyan adventure had drained much of Italy's resources, and its armed forces were not ready for any new challenges, especially from great powers.

On the other hand, some segments advocated war. One was the new nationalist movement that had blossomed at the turn of the century around the newspaper *L'idea nazionale* and the reviews *Leonardo, Il regno, Rivolta ideale*, and *La voce*. Its more political side, the Italian Nationalist Association, was led by Enrico Corradini and Alfredo Rocco, while Giovanni Papini and Giuseppe Prezzolini were more concerned with culture. The nationalist idea broadly embraced many intellectuals and writers, such as Gabriele d'Annunzio and those sympathetic to a cult of violence gaining popularity across Europe. They all heaped scorn on the sterile and exhausted Liberal Italy that could not offer them excitement and adventure.

Akin to the nationalists were some politically minded Futurists led by Filippo Marinetti, whose 1909 manifesto blared, "We want to glorify war, the sole hygiene of the world." They found a voice in Papini's and Ardegno Soffici's Florentine review, *Lacerba*, founded in 1913, which exalted the aesthetic roar of the machine and the beautiful explosions of bombs. The most grisly expression of this new violence may have been recorded by the nationalist Papini, who wrote, "[T]he future needs blood. It needs human victims, butchery. Internal war, and foreign war, revolution and conquest: that is history . . . blood is the wine of strong people, and blood is the oil for the great machine which flies from the past to the future." It cannot be said that such musings from artists and intellectuals were responsible for the war, but together they prepared a culture of violence that served its cause.

Despite the opposition and thanks in part to nationalists and Futurists, Prime Minister Salandra's government found a way to join the Great War. When the fighting started in 1914, his lofty protests of neutrality and those of Foreign Minister Antonio di San Giuliano (president of the Royal Italian Geographic Society) were promptly followed by secret talks with both warring sides for the best deal to bring Rome into the conflict. By the spring of 1915, Salandra rejected the last-ditch Hapsburg acquiescence to all of Italy's demands and instead opted to enjoy the greater rewards promised by Britain, France, and Russia. A deal, in fact, had already been struck with the entente on April 26, the Treaty of

London, which awarded to Italy Austria's territories of the Trentino and the South Tyrol, Gorizia, Trieste, Istria, and some islands and ports along the Dalmatian coast. Italy would also receive a war loan from Britain and a share of overseas lands, particularly from Austria's ally, the Ottoman Empire. Finally, the entente agreed to Rome's demand to exclude the pope from the peace conference.

The diplomatic stage was set but popular suspicions of war still needed to be overcome and Rome orchestrated a propaganda campaign under d'Annunzio's baton to prepare the way. The flamboyant poet led a chorus of nationalists, university students, Futurist artists and the interventionist renegade socialist Benito Mussolini to drum enough support to make the proclamation of war appear respectable. On May 4, 1915, Rome denounced the Triple Alliance and nineteen days later, on May 23, declared war on Austria-Hungary.

Kept in the dark most of the time, Italy's military was taken aback by the opening of hostilities. But it scored some surprising initial successes against the Austrians, pushing them back until Gorizia was taken in August 1916. The rugged Alpine terrain, however, impeded movement one way or the other, and the two sides battled over a largely stagnant line that mirrored the Western Front except for its higher altitude. Unlike in France, where a flat and muddy no-man's land separated the two sides, the Italians and the Austrians lobbed cannon and mortar shells at each other from high mountain perches across expansive valleys.

Leading the army was General Luigi Cadorna, son of the Piedmontese general who had breached Rome's walls in 1870. But the choice of the younger Cadorna to direct Italy's troops proved a tragic mistake. Without foresight or imagination, his insufferably imperious management debilitated and demoralized both officers and ranks. Cadorna could not take criticism and, from his headquarters at Udine, blamed all problems on politicians, particularly the minister of the interior, Vittorio Emanuele Orlando. Such was his contempt that, with the support of King Victor Emmanuel, he prohibited ministers from making the trip to the war zones.

Cadorna's treatment of front-line soldiers was wretched. Food rations barely provided energy, particularly in the cold alpine weather; pay was miserable; and entertainment was nonexistent except for his allowance for brothels and extra wine before battle. Consequently, as Martin Clark has written, Italy's "was a sullen, often illiterate, ill-equipped army, torn away from its homes and fields to fight on foreign soil for incomprehensible reasons."[4]

At home, Salandra's government was replaced in June 1916 by one headed by the president of the Dante Alighieri Society, Paolo Boselli. His was a cabinet of inclusion with Liberal stalwarts such as Vittorio Emanuele Orlando at the Interior Ministry, former Socialists Ivanoe Bonomi at Public Works and Leonida Bissolati as Minister without Portfolio, and a Catholic, Filippo Meda, at Finance. Military interference in civilian politics was also made apparent in the growing power of an emergency Ministry of Arms and Munitions. Headed by a general, it wielded broad powers over the wartime economy.

The war raised social resentments. Of the five million men drafted, most were peasants, men angered by what they considered preferential treatment accorded to skilled industrial workers who were needed on the home front to operate the booming war industries. Although less than half of these workers were draft-age men, industry expanded hand in hand with a growing labor shortage. FIAT, for example, a company whose production of trucks and other war matériel made it an essential industry, climbed from Italy's thirtieth largest manufacturing concern in 1914 to its fourth in 1918. It employed four thousand workers at the start of the war and forty thousand at its end. To satisfy the demand for labor, women assumed a larger and larger part of the industrial ranks. In wartime Turin, for example, they amounted to fifty-five thousand of the city's registered workforce of eighty-four thousand.

The war's strain eventually proved too great at the front, and in October 1917, the Italian line collapsed at Caporetto. Through the autumn rain and mud the army beat a chaotic retreat, while the Austrians, with massive numbers of German reinforcements, chased them west; 350,000 deserted, another 300,000 were taken prisoner. Cannon fire could be heard along the canals of Venice. The retreat continued until finally the troops rallied at the rain-swollen Piave River and checked the enemy's advance, between November 13 and 26, at the Battle of the Grappa near Belluno.

In Rome, Boselli's government crumbled even faster than did the front at Caporetto. The day after the first news of the disaster Boselli resigned. The Sicilian Vittorio Emanuele Orlando replaced him and soon received parliamentary support from another broad patriotic coalition of "National Defense." He coordinated political and military leaders in an extraordinary commission and replaced the detested Cadorna with Armando Diaz, a more pop-ular figure who paid attention to the welfare of his troops. Cen-sorship was relaxed at the front, and soldiers received more leave and better pay. Furthermore, the government established an agency, the Opera Nazionale Combattenti, to help soldiers and their families.

As the first anniversary of Caporetto approached in 1918, the Italians launched their own massive offensive along the Piave. They dealt the Austrians a crippling blow at Vittorio Veneto, and on November 3, Trent fell. That same day the two sides signed an armistice at the Villa Giusti near Padua. On the fourth a liberation flotilla appeared at Trieste harbor although the city had already freed itself. The war was over.

World War I was a disaster for Italy. Its official combat-death count was 571,000 soldiers. To this must be added 57,000 who died in prison camps and 60,000 missing. The conflict, moreover, shattered the premises that had guided Italy's Liberal elite since the Risorgimento. It marked the end of the dream that had driven leaders from Cavour to Giolitti and replaced it with a new reality of mass politics. It created a military-industrial state ruled by those with little interest in individual liberties or, for that mat-ter, Liberal institutions. Such monstrosities as the Ministry of Arms and Munitions, for instance, had never been seen before. The change that it and other emergency institutions introduced was so profound that the philosopher Benedetto Croce felt that

Mussolini did not kill Liberal Italy in 1922; rather, it died in 1915 when Rome declared war.

Notes

1. Benedetto Croce, *A History of Italy, 1871–1915* (New York: Atheneum, 1963), 214–15.

2. Giuliano Procacci, *History of the Italian People* (New York: Harper & Row, 1970), 129.

3. Ronald S. Cunsolo, *Italian Nationalism: From Its Origins to World War II* (Malabar, Fla.: Krieger, 1990), 219–20.

4. Martin Clark, *Modern Italy, 1871–1995* (London: Longman, 1996), 187.

Chapter 2
The Fascist Reformation

THE GREAT WAR shattered the Liberal dream for Italy, a vision replaced in 1922 by a new Fascist one that caught hold of the nation with astounding ferocity. When Benito Mussolini led about fifty followers to launch the Fascist movement in April 1919, few could have guessed that it would grow in three and a half years to become a major political force and capture the government in Rome. In the decades that followed, what Italians call the *ventennio* (twenty years), Mussolini and the Fascist regime attempted to remake the nation.

Fascism, however, was not the only contender in the struggle to supplant Liberalism. Other forces took aim at Italy's government that stood discredited from many angles. Nationalists launched a frontal assault on a government that they judged incapable of reaping any territorial benefits from the peace settlement. Many on the political Left considered Rome's trust in capital and management excessive and that the state sided with them too often against labor. This frustration escalated when postwar layoffs indicated that workers' sacrifices for the fatherland went unappreciated. Liberals and the moderate Left pinned great hopes on the reforming Francesco Saverio Nitti, whose cabinet replaced Vittorio

Emanuele Orlando's in June 1919 and lasted until the next summer. Prime Minister Nitti, however, lacked the strength and guile of the old standby, Giovanni Giolitti, and his inclination toward social reform bore little fruit. Giolitti returned to the office in June 1920, but the Left dismissed him at seventy-eight as either a relic or an enemy.

Versailles, the Nationalists, and d'Annunzio

Nationalists criticized Rome from a different perspective. Often gathered with Enrico Corradini's Italian Nationalist Association, which climbed to three hundred thousand members by 1922, they argued that the Liberal state, through spinelessness or treachery, missed totally the opportunities that the war presented. Although victorious, Rome failed to secure Italy's place in the sun with expanded borders in Europe and colonial booty beyond the sea. At home, moreover, the conservative nationalists resented the government's inability to control what they saw as leftist subversion.

Still, the peace settlements provoked most of the nationalists' ire. For them, Versailles meant shabby treatment from the Allies and reinforced Corradini's vision of Italy as a proletarian country, a have-not forced to witness but not partake of the banquet enjoyed by the wealthy nations. Another nationalist, the celebrity poet Gabriele d'Annunzio, declared that Versailles represented "decrepitude, infirmity, obtuseness, pain, cheating." The blood of hundreds of thousands of Italians seemed not to have mattered to their British and French allies who grabbed the German and Turkish colonial empires and then refused Rome's claims. The preachy discourses on national self-determination from U.S. president Woodrow Wilson, furthermore, and his insistence that France and Britain call their imperial aggrandizements mandates instead of colonies made postwar settlements appear even more rife with hypocrisy.

Problems posed by Italian demands in Asia and Africa were fairly simple. At the war's end Rome dispatched troops into

Turkey to consolidate its claims on Ottoman territories. They were joined by French, British, and Greek troops who landed there with the same purpose. But Mustafa Kemal's nationalist revolt and his struggle against the Greeks placed Rome in a difficult position. By June 1921, therefore, Italy and the other Allies abandoned Turkey although Britain and France retained their other acquisitions throughout the old empire's Middle Eastern regions. In Africa, on the other hand, Italy received what the powers considered compensation for sleights in other places. But compared to the Anglo-French feast on all of Germany's holdings there, extending Libya's southern frontier into empty deserts and Somalia's annexation of Jubaland only served to insult Italian nationalists.

In Europe, the peace accords raised different and more complicated issues. At first glance, the Allies appeared to yield to many of the nationalists' *irredentista* ambitions to liberate their Italian brothers and sisters from the Austrian yoke and join them to the fatherland. By pushing the border north to the Brenner Pass, for instance, Italy absorbed all of the Trentino and the Alto Adige, called the Sud Tirol by the Austrians, along with its mixed Italo-German population. In the East, the addition of Trieste, Gorizia, and Tarvisio with their Istrian and Slovene hinterlands repatriated Italians but also brought Slavs under the tricolor. Nationalists, moreover, could be relieved that Italy's neighbor to the east was no longer the formidable Austro-Hungarian Empire but the fledgling kingdom of Serbs, Croats, and Slovenes, later known as Yugoslavia.

Yugoslavia, however, held much of what Italy wanted. Rome's greatest conundrum concerned its claim to the coastal cities and islands of Dalmatia, an argument that pitted the Italians against an alliance of Serbs, Croats, Slovenes, and the great power representatives in Paris. Italian assertions rested on the legacy of almost one thousand years of Venetian rule over Dalmatia. Central to the issue was the former Austro-Hungarian port of Fiume. Identified by the Croats as Rijeka, the town had a considerable Italian population, while the surrounding countryside was more

Slav. At Versailles, Prime Minister Orlando had passionately im-
plored the Allies to recognize the city and the stretch of Adriatic
coastline as part of Italy. Wilson ignored these claims and supported the Yugoslav position, while the French and the British
hid behind the president to rein in the Italians.

Wilson's obstinate stand unleashed a fury of Italian denunciation
onto the head of the hapless Orlando, and his ministry collapsed.
His replacement by Nitti in June 1919, however, failed to improve
things. Nationalists considered the new government as a step backward; apprehensive that the new prime minister was even weaker
and more pliant than his predecessor, they feared that Nitti would
cave in and guarantee forever the detested Versailles provisions.

The time had come for many nationalists to quit waiting for
Rome and to seize the day themselves. On September 12, 1919,
d'Annunzio crossed the line and commanded a mixed corps of
active and discharged Italian soldiers in an invasion of Fiume, an
adventure intended to embarrass and topple the Nitti government. In what has been described as a "dress rehearsal for Fascism," the poet used Fiume as a stage from which he lambasted
Nitti's do-nothing ministry while acting the part of a Renaissance
condottiero, or mercenary. Replete with historic costumes and
ever-present Russian wolfhounds, d'Annunzio formed a government under the Charter of Carnaro and sustained it with dona-
tions from nationalist supporters, such as Mussolini, and from pi-
rate raids on the Adriatic. The greatest haul was the *Persia*, a
munitions ship headed for the relief of White Russians in their
civil war against the Bolsheviks. As the vessel sailed through the
Strait of Messina, the captain and crew, angry over shuttling aid to
Lenin's enemies, changed course in the direction of the poet's
renegade state. Fiume welcomed it with appropriate fanfare on
October 14.

In Rome, Nitti sat and suffered d'Annunzio's endless ridicule
from faraway Fiume, but his hands were tied. Had he chosen to
move against the popular warrior-bard and attack the Fiume "le-
gionnaires," Nitti might not have been able to rely on the loyalty
of his own soldiers. Would they fire on their Italian brothers?

Consequently, on June 15, 1920, Nitti's cabinet fell and was replaced by another under the more capable Giovanni Giolitti. The new prime minister and the Yugoslavs quickly patched things with the Treaty of Rapallo in November 1920. Fiume became a free state; Italy kept the Istrian peninsula, the coastal town of Zara, and a few Adriatic islands; while the Yugoslavs held the Fiume hinterland and the rest of Dalmatia. Four years later, Yugoslavia consented to Italian sovereignty over Fiume.

But what of d'Annunzio? By the time of the Rapallo agreement, most of Fiume's magic had worn off for him and for the Italian public. Giolitti knew he could simply dispatch a warship or two and deal the "Republic of Carnaro" a death blow. On Christmas Day 1920, therefore, the battleship *Andrea Doria* appeared off Fiume's shore and lobbed some well-placed shells into d'Annunzio's palace. The slightly wounded poet bemoaned "Bloody Christmas" but surrendered and returned to Italy ever the more popular. He had achieved his two purposes, those of discrediting the Italian government and of advertising himself.

Challenge from the Left

Fiume and the other challenges beyond Italy's borders paralleled domestic troubles. After the victory, the heat of wartime production quickly cooled and the economy unraveled, a situation complicated when the government's colossal debt triggered staggering inflation. Italy's currency, the lira, which cost U.S. 19.3¢ in 1913 (about five to the dollar), was revalued in 1919 to U.S. 4.97¢ (about twenty). By January 1921, a dollar cost almost thirty lire. The wholesale price index, marked at 100 in 1913, reached 590 by 1920. After the war, moreover, wages did not keep pace with prices but, in fact, fell. The bad times, furthermore, were not confined just to the workers. In 1921, two of Italy's largest corporations, Ansaldo and Ilva, went bankrupt. Such collapses, combined with production reconversions and cutbacks, were aggravated by large numbers of returning soldiers looking for work who sent the unemployment figures spiraling. In November 1919, the jobless figure peaked at two million.

The postwar situation presented opportunities to the political Left that seemed to grow in strength every day. The numbers validated this impression. Membership in the Socialist Party ballooned from 28,000 in 1918 to 216,000 in 1920, while its allied labor organization, the *Confederazione Generale di Lavoro* (CGL), shot from 250,000 in 1918 to over 2,000,000 in 1920. Such growth invited comparisons with Russia, where the old czarist empire had toppled and the provisional government then crumbled under the heel of the Bolsheviks. Parallels with Russia were not lost on those with interests in the status quo, those who grew more anxious with each passing day. For them the new black-shirted Fascists constituted a tough and aggressive group that might be relied on as enforcers and possibly even allies to take to the streets against the leftist menace.

Most observers, however, failed to realize that the Socialist threat would not last. Old rifts deepened between moderates and their more radical Maximalist comrades. The fissures had already been revealed at the 1912 Party Congress in Reggio nell'Emilia. There, the revolutionary wing that included the young Benito Mussolini had expelled a reformist faction led by Leonida Bissolati and Ivanoe Bonomi, whose support for the government's war effort in Libya triggered suspicion that the two had grown too friendly with the Roman establishment. After World War I, and despite Filippo Turati's exhortations against insurrection, the Russian Revolution inspired and emboldened the party's and the CGL's Maximalist leaders to press labor into a frenzy of strikes and calls for a voice in management. This agitation had its effect. Man-days lost to strikes skyrocketed from 906,000 in 1918 to 14.2 million in 1919. The 1919 Socialist Congress in Bologna accelerated attacks on the moderates and passed resolutions in favor of Moscow. The tactic paid off in the elections of that year when the party captured 156 seats in the chamber, more than any other.

Intransigent capitalists courted a confrontation with the workers and found it at Milan's Alfa Romeo plant. There, on August 30, 1920, management ordered a lockout against the particularly combative metallurgical union, the *Federazione Italiana Operai Metallurgici* (FIOM). Workers and unions retaliated with the occupation of three hundred factories, mainly in Milan and Turin, the "Petrograd of Italy." Workers' councils, or "soviets," emerged and some leaders pushed for the next step: proletarian revolution.

Prime Minister Giolitti responded with his usual cool head and ordered his police to patrol outside the factory gates but not to storm them. He reasoned that problems such as lack of technical and administrative know-how would confound the illegal occupants and their revolution would collapse on its own. Giolitti was right. The movement failed, and the occupations ended by late September. The revolutionary moment fizzled, and Socialists were left in bitter division. But Giolitti's public image suffered too, as a leader frozen in indecision.

Rancor persisted in the Socialist Party, which finally fell apart at its congress at Livorno in January 1921. Already in the summer of 1920 the Communist International, or Comintern, in Moscow had ordered the expulsion of all moderates from Marxist parties. The Maximalist majority of the Italian Party, however, proved reluctant to evict their old gradualist comrades. At Livorno, therefore, a strict Muscovite faction under Amedeo Bordiga and Antonio Gramsci dutifully led a revolt and founded a separate Communist Party of Italy (later, the Italian Communist Party). From the Livorno debacle, the angry Socialists branded their estranged Communist comrades as enemies. The last stage of the catastrophe occurred at the October 1922 Socialist Party Congress when the Maximalists and the Reformers finally split. Turati and Giacomo Matteotti left to form the Unitary Socialist Party (Partito Socialista Unitario, or PSU), which sought alliances with other democratic groups to fight the growing threat of Fascism.

Catholic Activity

Along with angry nationalists and the splintered Left, Catholic activists composed another group to challenge Italy's postwar Liberal state. On its far Left, the Catholic movement posed solutions as radical as any other. After the war, some Catholics opted for a "White Bolshevism" that mirrored Marxist action. This took the form of peasants led by "revolutionary" priests who invaded and occupied large expanses of fallow latifundia, largely in the south.

The 1919 elections, moreover, heralded the rise of an openly Catholic political party led by the Sicilian priest, Don Luigi Sturzo. Sturzo had resigned as head of the Catholic Action and in January 1919 established his new Popular Party (*Partito Popolare Italiano*, or PPI), at the Piazza Santa Chiara in Rome. The organization's twelve-point program called for the integrity of the family, social welfare and school reforms, guarantees for labor, and votes for women. It advocated a League of Nations, emphasized local and regional identities, promoted liberty of Christian conscience, and called for "full freedom of action for the Church's spiritual magisterium."[1]

Anxious that the PPI be considered a party for all Italians and not just the church's voice in politics, Sturzo carefully tread a path between the social radicals and the party's so-called clerical-moderate, or conservative wing. The Popular Party wanted to adopt, perhaps unrealistically, a multiclass look to embrace labor organizers as well as reactionary "black aristocrats" in Rome. It also frequently supported Nationalist positions abroad and backed d'Annunzio at Fiume despite the poet's expulsion of Catholic Croat priests from the city. The PPI tested its reach in the November 1919 vote and found the results encouraging. It captured 20.5 percent of the national tally, most of the peasant ballots, and large amounts among the middle class. This accounted for one hundred seats in the Chamber of Deputies. The party reaped even more votes in the 1921 elections, thanks in large part to ballots from the heavily Catholic Trentino region, which had been annexed from Austria.

But trouble at the Holy See jeopardized Don Sturzo's success. In 1922, Pope Benedict XV died and was succeeded by the archbishop of Milan, Achille Ratti, who took the name Pius XI. Born to a working-class family in 1857, Ratti served mainly in his native

Lombardy before 1910 when he was called to Rome for duties at the Vatican Library. His innate conservatism was reinforced by his brief career as papal diplomat, or apostolic visitor, and then as nuncio (ambassador) to Poland from 1918 to 1921. There he witnessed firsthand the struggle against Bolshevism, to the point that in the summer of 1920 he stayed in besieged Warsaw, risking capture by Lenin's Red Army. Pius believed in organizing the faithful in tight religious structures such as Catholic Action, but he suspected political activity of any sort. Later, when the Fascists' push came to shove, this pope could not be relied on to save the Popular Party.

The Rise of Fascism

Nationalist, Socialist, and Catholic opposition to Italy's Liberal government, however, was soon overwhelmed by another new political force: the Fascist movement led by the extraordinary personality of Benito Mussolini. Mussolini was a Romagnole, born in 1883 in the town of Predappio near Forlì. His father, Alessandro, was true to Romagna's revolutionary traditions, an anarchist who bounced among his blacksmith's job, prison, and the tavern. Benito's mother, Rosa, was a schoolteacher and a devout Catholic who, it has been said, provided him with stability during his early years. After some tumultuous school terms, the young Mussolini worked briefly as a teacher before leaving for Switzerland in 1902. Many reasons have been presented for his emigration, including draft evasion and skipping out on the rent. The rudderless Mussolini tramped around, took odd jobs, got arrested, and latched onto revolutionary circles in Lausanne. By 1905, he returned to Italy to serve his time in the army thanks to an amnesty proclaimed for draft evaders.

Mussolini soon gravitated toward journalism and politics. He wrote for and edited Socialist newspapers and acquired a reputation, not only as a competent journalist but as a firebrand who challenged the party's reformist leadership. His temper did not hurt his career, and he rose quickly in the party ranks. At the Socialist Congress of 1912, Mussolini participated in the successful expulsion of Bissolati and Bonomi for their support of Italy's war against the Ottoman Empire, efforts that netted him the editor's chair of the party organ, *Avanti!*

World War I turned Mussolini's world on its head. It led to a rupture between him and his Socialist comrades who stood for a neutral Italy. Mussolini, instead, promoted entrance into the conflict as a revolutionary act that would push the nation closer to authentic class struggle. Consequently, the Socialist executives pressured him from his editorship and ostracized him from their ranks. Estranged from the party although his socialist beliefs were still fervid, if unorthodox, the journalist quickly acquired the reputation of an interventionist. Kindred factions took notice and supported his ambitions to found a new paper. With French and Russian money as well as funds from the Bolognese daily, the *Resto del Carlino*, various industrialists, and the Italian government, Mussolini realized his dream. In Milan, he gave birth to his own journal, *Il popolo d'Italia*, the newspaper that years later would become the official organ of the Fascist regime. It was November 1914, only a month after he had left *Avanti!*

Mussolini still considered himself a man of the Left, but, as one biographer has written, his "new hero was not Marx but Mazzini, who dreamt of a patriotic war to secure Italy's 'natural frontiers' of language and race."[2] To set an example and perhaps to prove his own worth to himself, Mussolini enlisted and joined the troops at the front. He served there with distinction until he suffered severe wounds during a training exercise and was honorably discharged. Out of the hospital and back in Milan, Mussolini exhorted victory and nationalism in the pages of *Il popolo d'Italia* and raised eyebrows as a man to watch.

In the highly charged political atmosphere of postwar Italy, Mussolini created a movement based on the belief that outdated Liberal and Marxist solutions were inadequate for Italy's quandary. New and audacious ideas were necessary. On March 23, 1919, the first meeting of Mussolini's *Fasci di Combattimento* took place at a hall in Milan's Piazza San Sepolcro. Since at least the *Fasci Siciliani* rebellions of the last century, the word *fascio* (*fasci* is the plural) had signified an engaged group of any stripe across the political spectrum. But after 1919, Mussolini and his followers would forever own the word. Fascism's first platform, released in June, was an odd convergence of Left and Right—of nationalist aims, anti-Communism, workers' participation in management, tax reform, abolition of the monarchy and the senate, women's suffrage, confiscation of church property, "economic democracy," and an attack on war profiteers. Recognizing some contradictions, the *Popolo d'Italia* declared, "We allow ourselves the luxury of being aristocrats and democrats, conservatives and progressives, reactionaries and revolutionaries, legalists and anti-legalists."[3]

The 1919 platform illustrates that from the beginning, Fascism lacked a precise definition, and debates over its meaning persist into the twenty-first century. Part of the problem is the confusion of "capital *F*" *Fascist*, the strictly Italian phenomenon, with the "lowercase *f*" generic form that has been applied to radical Right associations and ideas around the world. To organize a worldwide solidarity, for example, in the early 1930s fascists, or those who called themselves fascists, created their own "international," as the Marxists had done in the nineteenth century. They failed, however, to reach a workable definition that embraced them all. Part of the problem was Italian Fascism's tendency to evolve in sometimes contradictory directions between 1919 and the end of World War II in 1945. Mussolini's early platforms that revealed traces of leftist rhetoric, for example, were jettisoned toward 1922 as he and his legions marched farther to the Right. What, then, was, or is, Fascism? Does (or did) a generic fascism exist that can be applied to other nations?

Some have dismissed Fascism as little or nothing more than a vehicle to take power and keep it for its leader. It was Mussolinism, or *ducismo*, a term that pertains to Mussolini's adopted title, *Duce*. In March 1923, the Duce declared his intention to govern with as broad a consensus as possible. But, he continued, until that concord was attained, he would accumulate "the greatest amount of force available. Because it may be that force will lead to consensus and, in any event, should consensus be lacking, force is there."[4] Beyond brutality, however, in a very broad sense Fascism embraced nationalist and authoritarian principles. Other movements and regimes, however, few of which could be considered fascist, have also claimed these ideas.

Nor was Mussolini Europe's first right-wing dictator. Alexander Stamboliski's government in Bulgaria from 1919 until 1923 and Admiral Miklos Horthy's regime in Hungary were both rightist and authoritarian. Nevertheless, distinctions separated him and those who came before him. More than those precursors, the former editor of *Avanti!* was not afraid of socialism, and aspects of it found a home in his regime. One historian has calculated, moreover, that, like the Duce himself, seven of the top fourteen Fascists came to the movement from the political Left; of Mussolini's 136 federal secretaries, 37 began their political lives on the Left; and 22 had been members of Masonic orders.

At the end of his life, furthermore, Mussolini revisited his socialist roots in an attempt to expand the working-class voice in commerce and industry. The experiment was doomed in that the Fascists would direct from above this proletarian revolution, and most workers refused to buy what he was selling. Yet even earlier, during the regime's salad days, the Duce used his power to provide the Italians with a welfare state far more comprehensive than anything the Liberals had devised before 1922. And so the grafting of welfare provisions to nationalist authoritarianism was embodied in Fascism, a blend of themes recalled in the Italian joke about a son pestering his father at the dinner table. To the boy's insistence on a definition of Mussolini's state, the father retorted, "Eat and shut up!" a simple expression that seemed to embody the essence of Fascism.

Fascism's first halting forays into politics met with disappointment. From the fifty or so adherents at the Piazza San Sepolcro in March 1919, the group expanded to only 870 by December. Particularly depressing for Mussolini were the November elections in which his list lost across the board. In Milan, a coalition of Fascists, Futurists, and discharged *Arditi* shock troops reaped less than 5,000 votes out of 270,000. It seemed that Mussolini's young movement had reached a premature death. For many stalwarts, however, disappointment at the polls justified adoption of more outrageous and violent tactics.

Fascists turned to violence as their ally in Italy's public square. Many assembled in the ranks of the *squadristi*, street fighters who acquired the habits of wearing black shirts and carrying weapons to bully "bolsheviks" and anyone else who got in their way. Their motto of "*me ne frego*" ("I don't give a damn") fit their swagger. Mussolini set an example for these radicals by keeping hand grenades and daggers at his editor's desk at the *Popolo d'Italia*. The raucous *squadrista* style alienated elements of the sober middle classes, but it also attracted others who felt that a good street thrashing was just the thing for Marxist miscreants. The movement found sympathizers in important figures such as Giolitti and the ex-Socialist Bonomi, who followed him as prime minister from July 1921 until February 1922. While they rejected Mussolini's philosophy, they nevertheless felt that his movement could be used to their advantage with little deleterious impact on the Italian body politic. Watch the Fascists, Giolitti counseled—they will be like a firecracker: a big boom, followed by just a bit of smoke. This impression proved to be a costly mistake.

Despite their electoral setbacks, the Fascists scored points elsewhere, as mercenaries and hired guns against leftists, Catholic activists, and ethnic minorities. Factory owners in Milan and Turin and Po valley landholders quickly valued blackshirt willingness and ability to battle subversives. Strike breaking, street brawls, and raids on farm workers became part of the Fascist identity. Nationalists, particularly, applauded Fascist attacks on Italy's new minority populations. It was no coincidence that some of *squadrismo*'s earliest victories occurred in the northeast, along the volatile Yugoslav border. Most estimates claim that about two thousand people lost their lives in the years of street fighting before Mussolini took office. Blackshirt deaths accounted for about a quarter of that number.

By the end, of 1921 the movement had evolved into a political party with 220,000 adherents. A survey of 150,000 of these revealed one-half as war veterans. Twenty-four percent were farm workers, while about twenty thousand were students. And the ranks continued to expand. By January 1922, the Fascist labor societies under Edmondo Rossoni claimed another five hundred thousand members; and in May, party cards reached over three hundred thousand Italians.

Contrasted to Mussolini's success, anti-Fascist resistance crumbled. In an ill-timed show of strength, a broad alliance of left-wing labor forces led by the reformist Socialists called a general strike on July 31, 1922. The gambit proved disastrous. Few workers joined the walkout, and the Fascists gained political capital from it by commandeering idle transport and utilities and running them for the public good.

Throughout this period, furthermore, the Fascists launched a campaign to capture local power, aggressions that took place almost entirely in northern Italy. The first assault occurred in September 1921 when, recalling d'Annunzio at Fiume, the Duce's lieutenant, Italo Balbo, led a march on Ravenna. He occupied the city long enough to throttle enemies and burn down some "subversive" buildings. This slapdash affair of random violence inspired Balbo to note, "For the first time then I had a sense of the future possibilities."[5] Balbo followed with another raid on Ferrara in May 1922. There, he occupied the city for two days until he received government guarantees for an effective public works program. A week later, the Fascists held Bologna for five days; in July, Roberto Farinacci took Cremona's city hall. On July 29, the irrepressible Balbo led a "column of fire" on a rampage through Romagna. Inspired by victory after victory over the disorganized Left and the paralyzed government, Mussolini realized that his chance had come to put his machine to the highest test. On October 24, at a huge public rally in Naples, the Duce called for a Fascist march on Rome.

Blackshirts from all over Italy heeded the clarion and within hours began to assemble in camps that circled the capital. From

Milan, Mussolini directed operations with one eye on an escape route into Switzerland. Closer to Rome, his comrades secured Perugia and established their forward command there. While about seventy thousand soaked in autumnal downpours and waited for marching orders, reaction came from the government of Luigi Facta. A lackluster lawyer of the Giolitti faction who headed a stop-gap cabinet, Facta urged King Victor Emmanuel III to halt the march with a proclamation of martial law. Marshal Diaz and the army were prepared to confront the Fascists, and a show of force would have been sufficient against the haphazard and poorly armed Fascists. But, as at Fiume, to fire on so many Great War veterans undoubtedly gave pause, and the king decided at the last moment against the order. His judgment was taken so late that some of Facta's martial law proclamations had already gone up around Rome.

Instead, on October 29, 1922, Victor Emmanuel invited the thirty-nine-year-old Mussolini to form a cabinet. The monarch's first choice had been Antonio Salandra, who offered Mussolini a cabinet position. But the Duce refused, and Salandra then suggested that the king approach the Fascist to head the government. Mussolini arrived from Milan on the morning of October 30 to lead the, by now, inconsequential march on Rome. The revolution had been averted to the disappointment of many blackshirts who still itched for a little adventure and wished for a real attack on the capital. During the march, therefore, they pretended to storm Rome by shooting their guns into the air, beating up enemies, setting some buildings on fire, and killing twelve people.

The Fascists in Power

Despite the big show and without the advantage of hindsight, few in 1922 could have predicted any really profound consequences of the "March on Rome." Mussolini's authoritarian state did not spring full-blown from the Duce's brain. It developed over time. Prime Minister Mussolini was a Fascist, but he did not begin his

tenure as a dictator. Victor Emmanuel still sat on the throne, and
the new government was not particularly out of the ordinary: a
Center–Right coalition with (including the prime minister) only
four Fascists. That the entire cabinet did not wear black shirts, in
fact, angered many Fascist Party lieutenants who had been excluded. Instead of them, two Catholic Popolari were chosen, as
were four Liberals, the normal service ministers, Marshal Armando Diaz at the Ministry of War and Admiral Paolo Thaon di
Revel at the Ministry of the Navy, and some Nationalists. At the
Ministry of Education, Mussolini chose Giovanni Gentile, a figure
who would later be identified second only to the Duce as the
regime's philosopher. In February 1923, moreover, the Nationalist
Association would merge with the Fascists as one party, the Partito Nazionale Fascista (PNF).

One of the first indications of things to come was the 1923 electoral legislation crafted by Giacomo Acerbo, Mussolini's undersecretary of state. To the party with the most popular votes and at
least 25 percent of the tally, the so-called Acerbo Law would award
two-thirds of the chamber's 535 seats. Challenged by the Socialists
and the Catholics, the bill relied on Fascist and most of the Liberal votes to pass on July 15. The following April, Mussolini held
elections wherein he and his allies swamped the opposition with
over 66 percent of the vote. As it turned out, he was able to assemble his parliamentary juggernaut without the Acerbo Law.

But the authoritarian state still had a long way to go before it
came together. The Matteotti affair, more than any other event,
provided Mussolini with the opportunity to establish his dictatorship. Giacomo Matteotti was a reformist socialist (PSU) deputy
who denounced the Fascists from the chamber floor on May 30,
1924. He declared that he could discredit the blackshirts with
proof of fraud at the polls and other misdeeds. On June 10, Matteotti vanished, the victim of blackshirt hotheads in search of re-
venge. His remains were discovered over two months later, and
everything pointed to the Fascists.

The crisis paralyzed the Duce. The press carried on a campaign
against him, most of his Liberal allies deserted, and even some

moderate Fascists tore up their party cards. In Parliament, one hundred enraged anti-Fascist deputies led by the Liberal Giovanni Amendola walked out of the chamber. The action was doomed to failure because the largest opposition faction had just neutralized itself in righteous indignation.

In the end, Fascism's radical wing, led by Roberto Farinacci, pressured Mussolini to respond. On December 31, 1924, the group met with the prime minister and convinced him to make up his mind and employ the trusted *squadristi* to crack down on the opposition with a "second wave" of blackshirt violence. Only then could he relaunch Fascism without his establishment allies. Mussolini had tamed the squads in 1923 by submerging them into his personal army, the Fascist Militia (*Milizia Volontaria per la Sicurezza Nazionale*, or MVSN). Now more professionally armed and attired, the MVSN nevertheless remained a haven for rowdy Fascist street fighters, loyal to the Duce but bored with drills and ceremony.

Before Parliament, on January 3, 1925, an emboldened Mussolini dared the opposition to remove him and launched his second wave of creating a new Italy. The Duce relied on his minister of justice, the ex-Nationalist Alfredo Rocco, to draft many of the seminal decrees aimed at consolidating his dictatorship and constructing the Fascist state. As Norberto Bobbio wrote, "the storm of tyranny broke over Italy."[6] Within two days, the Duce ordered the arrest of 111 opponents and launched a crusade against the free press. He had already crafted a censorship decree in 1923 but had quashed it to appease the Liberals. Now Mussolini ordered his prefects to resurrect the law and apply it. Many papers simply caved in by firing editors and staff members whom the Fascists considered offensive. The "Press Law of December 31, 1925" then formally muzzled the newspapers by creating a Fascist board to license journalists. By November 1926, Italy's free press ceased to exist.

Mussolini also targeted the political opposition. The 1924 elections and the disastrous decision to walk out of the legislature to protest the Matteotti affair had already weakened the other parties.

Most who had absented themselves were simply barred from reentering the Parliament. Mussolini then turned to eliminate all rival political parties. The first to fall was the Socialist PSU, the party of Turati and Matteotti. One from their ranks, Tito Zaniboni, attempted to shoot Mussolini in October 1925, and the government reacted immediately by banning the PSU.

The Fascists needed little effort to destroy the Popular Party, which had already started to crack on its own. The Catholic "clerical-moderates" of its right wing, contributed to their party's dissolution when they launched an exodus into Fascist ranks. Just as damaging were the actions of the Holy See. A party so associated with the church ran a great risk in that, whether they liked it or not, the Popolari depended on Pope Pius's goodwill, a commodity that ran out by the end of 1924. Prospects of a Socialist–Catholic alliance over the Matteotti affair had pushed the pontiff too far, and he began to withdraw his papal cover from the party. To a student group in September, Pius questioned the wisdom of unnecessary political activity among Catholics. Then, a month later, the Popolari lost their leader when the Holy See ordered Don Sturzo to retire from politics and leave Italy. The last PPI congress, chaired by Don Sturzo's successor, Alcide De Gasperi, convened in June 1925. *Il popolo*, the party organ, closed in November, and De Gasperi resigned in December.

All semblance of open politics in Italy ended when the "Exceptional Decrees" of November 1926 banned all opposition organizations. At the same time, the Fascists annulled the 120 seats in the Chamber that had remained empty since Amendola's "Aventine Secession" and created a Special Tribunal for the Defense of the State to try political offenses. For enforcement, however, the Fascists relied on neighborhood informants and on the police network that the Liberals had already built in the Ministry of the Interior. Even the Fascist secret police, the OVRA, was no more than an expanded edition of the ministry's old unit. And Mussolini's police boss, Arturo Bocchini, was a staid civil servant who had begun his career before the March on Rome.

While Mussolini and the Fascists must be held accountable for their crimes, compared to the monstrous records of Europe's other interwar dictatorships, the Italian police state was almost benign. Throughout the entire history of the regime, about five thousand people received sentences for political crimes, while ten thousand were sent to *confino*, often a sort of house arrest in a far-off village, a strange existence recalled in Carlo Levi's classic account, *Christ Stopped at Eboli*. Until 1940, only nine executions were carried out, largely against Slovene separatists. As one historian has commented, the regime "was brutal and oppressive, but not murderous and bloodthirsty."[7]

Every opposition leader had a different story after 1926. Filippo Turati was secretly rescued by the Rosselli brothers, Carlo and Sandro, and smuggled out of Italy in a motorboat. The Fascists jailed the Catholic De Gasperi before he could flee, and he remained incarcerated until 1929 when he found employment in the safety of the Vatican Library. The Communist leader Amedeo Bordiga was also arrested and condemned to prison until 1930. His comrade Antonio Gramsci was arrested on November 8, 1926, and served time in Fascist jails until his release in 1937. Physically broken, he died only three days later. In 1926, the Liberals Giovanni Amendola and Piero Gobetti both perished in France after severe beatings at the hands of the blackshirts. Finally, the old prime minister, Giovanni Giolitti, tolerated but virtually alone in Parliament, spoke out against Mussolini one last time before his death from natural causes on July 17, 1928.

Political organizations that challenged the regime generally had to flee Italy and regroup elsewhere. Gathered first in France and later in the United States, they fragmented into three groups: the largely Socialist "Anti-Fascist Concentration," Carlo Rosselli's progressive "Justice and Liberty," and a Communist faction under Moscow's direction. Other individuals such as Gaetano Salvemini and Carlo Sforza worked against Mussolini's dictatorship. The most important clandestine activity within Italy was a skeleton organization centered in Milan and maintained by the Communists.

The Fascist Regime

Perhaps Mussolini saw little need to adopt more vicious methods against his enemies because his control was effective where it counted. The regime had dealt death blows to rival political parties and to their journals. It crippled free and organized labor in the Vidoni Pact of October 1925 through which corporate leaders agreed to recognize and deal only with Fascist unions.

But there were limits to the Duce's control, limits that he accepted at least for the time being. Big business, the Catholic Church, the Crown, and the royalist military maintained certain freedoms of actions. The Duce could usually cajole and coerce them into cooperation when he needed to, and serious disputes surfaced only rarely. But his inability to gain full control of those conservative forces would return to haunt him. The source of his undoing in 1943 would be found not in the defeated Left but in this co-opted Right.

Perhaps because of his faulty domination of the Italian elite, Mussolini made more of an effort to reach and win the masses. To embrace and control them, the Fascists created scores of organizations. The Fasci Femminili, for instance, were Fascist women's auxiliaries established in 1920. They maintained a narrow, upper middle-class character, however, and more women were affected by another organization, the government's National Agency for Maternity and Childhood (*Opera Nazionale per la Maternità ed Infanzia*, or ONMI), established in 1925 for maternity assistance and employed in 1927 in the state's unsuccessful drive to increase birthrates. In the 1930s, more groups appeared to organize and control urban working women and peasants. Other unions organized professors, lawyers, blue-collar workers, railroad employees, and about anyone else in the social fabric who enrolled in Fascist organizations.

The party itself sat at the top, trying to maintain its pretensions as the nation's political elite. The PNF pin could provide a leg up to Italians with ambitious career hopes, and restricted membership allowed the Fascists take care of their own. The ideal way to

enter party ranks was through a progression of societies that fit-
ted the young for adult black shirts. The first step in this sanctioned development of young Fascists took place at the age of six
with the "Children of the She-Wolf." The *Opera Nazionale Balilla*
(changed to *Gioventù Italiana del Littorio* in 1937) was founded in
1926 to coordinate all youth groups while enrolling eight- to four-
teen-year-old boys. Girls from eight to twelve years of age entered
the *Piccole Italiane*. At fifteen, boys entered the "Avant-garde"
(*Avanguardisti*), while girls went into the *Giovani Italiane*. At
eighteen the university elite prepared itself for the blackshirt life
in the *Gioventù Universitaria Fascista*, while the rest went into the
Fasci Giovanili di Combattimento. By the 1930s, these party organizations submitted to government sanction and control
through the Ministry of National Education. Traditional Italian
roles between male and female surfaced in some of the rituals.
Boys marched with guns (or sticks if the cost was too much for
their families), while girls paraded holding dolls. But regardless of
sex, all took an oath to follow the Duce and to serve "with all
[their] strength and, if necessary, [their] blood the Cause of the
Fascist Revolution."[8]

Central to Fascism's popular organization was work. Although
political parties and independent workers' unions had been dissolved, wages dropped, and a police state instituted, Mussolini
hailed his labor system as an integral part of his corporate idea.
The corporate state was Fascism's most innovative and elaborate
vision of governance, and it was perhaps the regime's greatest ideological failure. The Duce hoped to reorganize Italy's society,
economy, and state by applying to them what he called corporatist
principles. Derived from a mix of syndicalist thought, Mussolini's
authoritarianism, and medieval Catholic tradition, his aim on
paper was to establish self-governing associations of workers and
employers. Divided according to occupations and industries,
these agencies would be managed by the Fascists at the apex of the
state.

In 1926, Alfredo Rocco's "Law for the Judicial Regulation of
Labor Disputes" supplied the first steps toward the corporate state

and the establishment of a Ministry of Corporations. In 1927, one of the regime's chief intellectuals, Giuseppe Bottai, composed the "Charter of Labor" to define the aims of the corporate movement. "Work," it read, "in all its forms—intellectual, technical and manual—both organizing or executive, is a social duty. . . . From the national standpoint the mass of production represents a single unit; it has a single object, namely the well-being of individuals and the development of national power."[9]

In 1929, Bottai became the minister of corporations and guided the program through its most ambitious phase. His plans could be implemented in part because the world economic crisis began to affect Italy after 1929 and cut industry's ability to challenge Fascist legislation. Consequently, the National Council of Corporations was established in March 1930 as a sort of economic legislature for seven newly created organs, those of industry, agriculture, banking, internal navigation, commerce, sea and air transport, and the arts.

The Fascists subsequently created more corporate bodies although by 1934 the steam had run out of the experiment. In 1939, the last manifestation of the program was to replace the Chamber of Deputies with a Chamber of Fasces and Corporations. The Italian Parliament, however, was by that time a dead letter anyway, and so was the corporate state. Only a formidable bureaucracy remained along with the memory of Fascism's economic "third way."

Hierarchy was another guiding principle of the Fascist state. *Gerarchia* (Hierarchy) was, in fact, the title of the party's principal review. The natural ranking of leaders over the population and obedience to their authority were openly elitist principles gladly embraced by the Fascists. Two of the regime's mottos, stenciled on the sides of buildings all over Italy, emphasized that the Duce was the leader and demanded that the people follow him: "Mussolini is always right" and "Believe, Obey, Fight!" At the top of the pile stood Mussolini, and an appropriate cult evolved to exalt him as a superman, a genius, the man of providence, and the greatest Italian of them all.

Around the Duce, Fascism created a galaxy of lesser lights, the *gerarchi*, who orbited Mussolini's sun. They were a diverse lot. A select few, Emilio De Bono, Cesare de Vecchi, Italo Balbo, and Michele Bianchi, were accorded special prestige as the Quadrumviri who led the March on Rome with Mussolini in 1922. This title was honorific, however, and the Quadrumviri gained nothing tangible from it. Being a Quadrumvir did not, for instance, save De Bono from execution by Mussolini's firing squad in 1944. Figures such as Roberto Farinacci, Dino Grandi, and Balbo were *gerarchi* who had emerged in the turbulent early years as *squadrista* leaders. Others, such as Edmondo Rossoni or Bianchi, came from the labor movement, while Costanzo Ciano and Giuseppe Volpi represented business interests friendly to the Fascists. Identified with other currents in Italian society were leaders such as Cesare De Vecchi, for example, who maintained close links to the Crown and the church. Giuseppe Bottai started as a futurist, and Luigi Federzoni came from Nationalist ranks. Many *gerarchi* also identified closely with their roles as provincial leaders. Farinacci, for example, was the boss, or *ras*, of Cremona. De Vecchi controlled the Turin organization, and Ferrara was Balbo's turf. Mussolini, the *gerarchi*, and the party would lead a revolution of minds and hearts that would reach into every corner of the nation. "I am deeply convinced," wrote the Duce in 1932, that Italy's "way of eating, dressing, working and sleeping, the entire complex of our daily habits must be reformed."[10]

Arts under Fascism

The art world illustrated some of the difficulties as well as the successes of Mussolini's attempts to create a Fascist Italy. Many of the same artistic revolutions that overwhelmed all of postwar Europe were also experienced in Italy during the *ventennio*. The early 1920s were marked by the deaths of the composer Giacomo Puccini and the world-famous tenor Enrico Caruso. Other prominent artists built, or rested, on reputations earned before the Fascists came to power. Gabriele d'Annunzio assumed the mantle of Italy's poet laureate and retired to his temple of decadence, the "Vittoriale," on Lake Garda's shore. Considered "a living monument to his former self" by one historian, he received from the Duce a special party card and the prow of the cruiser, *Puglia.* d'Annunzio placed the truncated ship on his lawn and fired its cannons for distinguished guests.

On the other hand, artists and scholars of international fame such as the Nobel Prize–winning playwright Luigi Pirandello and the painter Giorgio De Chirico continued their work into the 1920s with hardly a nod to the blackshirts. The Liberal philosopher, Benedetto Croce, was even left alone, although, despite his 1925 "Manifesto of Anti-Fascist Intellectuals," in the oppressive atmosphere that followed it, he turned to more purely academic pursuits. Like that of Pirandello and De Chirico, Croce's international reputation guaranteed that the Duce would leave him unmolested as long as he stayed away from his turf. In 1929, to sweeten the mixture, Mussolini courted or co-opted many of Italy's leading men of letters and sciences, by establishing the Royal Academy. Membership immortalized such luminaries as the composer Pietro Mascagni and the scientist Guglielmo Marconi. One year before his death, the aged d'Annunzio became its president in 1937.

In architecture, modern styles blended easily in the works of Giuseppe Pagano and Marcello Piacentini. Pagano's Casa del Fascio in Como and his Santa Maria Novella Railroad Station in Florence, furthermore, provided noteworthy evidence that, unlike Hitler, Mussolini did not reject the modern style. One can still contemplate Piacentini's more heavy-handed visions of Fascist Rome's inheritance from the Caesars in his remarkable structures at *Esposizione Universale di Roma* (EUR), the site of the regime's aborted 1942 World's Fair and today one of the capital's most bustling suburbs.

In music, the loss of Puccini in 1924 left Ottorino Respighi as Italy's premier composer. He was the most significant member of the "Generation of '80," the self-conscious group of composers born between 1875 and 1885 that included Alfredo Casella, Gian Francesco Malipiero, Franco Alfano, and Riccardo Zandonai.

Another figure, not noted as a composer but Italy's most famous musician of the age, was Arturo Toscanini. He also represented the problems that the regime posed for many in the art community. After the Great War, Mussolini's young movement had attracted Toscanini, he had conducted for d'Annunzio and his legionaires at Fiume, and he was even persuaded to place his name on the ill-fated electoral list of November 1919. But his feelings for Fascism had soured by the time Mussolini came to power, and, as early as December 1922, Toscanini courted blackshirt wrath by refusing to lead the party marching song, "Giovinezza," at Milan's La Scala Theater.

Although he did not sign Croce's manifesto of anti-Fascist intellectuals, Toscanini reached the breaking point with the regime by the mid and late 1920s. He retired from La Scala in 1928 and increasingly appeared abroad, particularly with the New York Philharmonic and, later, the NBC Symphony. On May 14, 1931, however, Toscanini was in Italy to lead the orchestra of Bologna's Teatro Comunale. His refusal to open the concert with "Giovinezza" had become the buzz around the city. As the conductor entered the theater, he met with a gang of blackshirts who pummeled him until friends came to his rescue. In 1938, Toscanini left Italy and refused to return until after Mussolini was gone.

Mussolini's interest in cultural politics extended to an appreciation of radio and film. Although wireless transmissions were invented by the Bolognese inventor Guglielmo Marconi, regular programming did not begin in Italy until 1924. By 1939, however, about one million receivers hummed across the nation. To regulate radio, the Fascists allowed a private consortium, the *Unione Radiofonica Italiana* (URI), to control broadcasting. In 1927, the URI became the Ente Italiano Audizione Radiofoniche (EIAR), which submitted to Mussolini's interference as he turned to focus more attention on the industry.

The Italian cinema had been established before World War I, and although its international reputation suffered during the conflict, it continued in a more modest form afterward. For film, the Fascists established *L'Unione Cinematografica Educativa* (LUCE) in 1927, but only for newsreels and documentaries and not for the production of entertainment films, which remained mostly in private hands. The regime neither controlled nor commanded filmmakers in the manner that the Soviet state could and did. The cinema industry, indeed, received no state funds until the early 1930s. Consequently, film censorship was not rigorous until the middle of the decade.

Control tightened when Mussolini created the Ministry of Press and Propaganda in 1935 and transformed it two years later into the Ministry of Popular Culture. Still, for every clear or thinly disguised propaganda piece such as Carmine Gallone's epic *Scipio l'Africano* (1937), Italy produced far more so-called white telephone films: sentimental pastiches, love stories, and frothy fun. Just like their American, French, or British counterparts, Italian moviegoers demanded comedies, action stories, and romance. The huge portion of Italian screen time devoted to foreign, particularly American films, in fact, illustrated the regime's tenuous grip on popular culture. An experimental film center (*Centro Sperimentale Cinematografico*) was founded near Cinecittà, the Roman "Hollywood," to explore and innovate in the medium. Its activity was often far removed from official film culture and trained many post- and anti-Fascist filmmakers such as Michelangelo Antonioni and Roberto Rossellini.

The Holy See also clipped Fascist hopes at cultural hegemony by inaugurating Radio Vaticana in 1931 and through Catholic newsreels distributed across the country via the Church's gigantic network of parish theaters. The newspaper voice of the Holy See, *L'osservatore romano*, furthermore, enjoyed complete freedom of circulation throughout most of the Fascist era as did the Jesuit review, *La civiltà cattolica*. Clear alternative voices, therefore, circulated publicly in Italy despite whatever may have been Mussolini's wishes.

The Church and the Lateran Accords

More than any institution, the Catholic Church represented the hardest nut to crack for Mussolini. Other segments of Italian society maintained some freedom of movement under the Fascists. The Savoy monarchy and the aristocracy, the military, and big business all held a degree of independence stained by compromise with the regime. The church compromised as well. But the Holy See headed a global organization with enormous international prestige. It also counted on the loyalty of Italy's faithful who constituted the vast majority of the population. These factors gave Pope Pius XI the ability to pass judgment on the Fascists that others could not match.

On the other hand, the Fascist regime held the keys to two prizes coveted by the church. The first was land. Since 1870, the pontiff had remained a "prisoner of the Vatican" whose territories had been stolen by Italy's secular government. Many Catholics welcomed the fact that the pope was no longer a temporal ruler but also worried that an Italian government, Liberal or Fascist, could curtail his freedom as a religious figure. The old Liberal state possessed the ability to make life difficult for parishes, clergy, and the religious. During the nineteenth century, it had infringed on the church's role in schools, it had jailed priests, and it confiscated much of the church's property. If anything, the Fascists could be even more unscrupulous than their Liberal predecessors. Creating an independent territory, therefore, no matter how small, might enable the church to achieve its second aim, freedom of action—freedom to work among the Italian people and on the international stage.

The Holy See, therefore, reached a reconciliation with the Italian government in the Lateran Accords of 1929. Steps toward the accommodation had already begun before World War I. In the face of expanding Socialist influence, in 1904 Pius X relaxed the *Non expedit* that prohibited Catholic votes and allowed the faithful to join the body politic in ever-increasing numbers. The Great War united church and state further in the form of chaplains and of religious women who staffed the military hospitals. Throughout the 1920s, the church moved closer and closer to the state through connections in the Vatican-owned Bank of Rome and individuals such as Cesare de Vecchi and Francesco Pacelli, brother of the future Pope Pius XII. The church had stood alongside Mussolini during the Matteotti crisis, and in 1924, Pius XI thanked God for sparing the Duce's life after an assassination attempt. Pius's defusing of the Popolare party in the mid-1920s, furthermore, saved the Duce potential trouble and was paid back in measures to increase clergy salaries, outlaw Masonic organizations, and reintroduce the crucifix to walls in public buildings. The cynical Romagnole revolutionary even legitimized his own marriage, and children, in 1925 through a church wedding. Negotiations for an Italo–Vatican accommodation opened in 1926.

On February 11, 1929, Mussolini and the pope's secretary of state, Cardinal Pietro Gasparri, signed a treaty, a financial convention, and a concordat known collectively as the Lateran Accords. These documents recognized a sovereign Vatican state that covered a parcel of Rome around St. Peter's basilica along with some other churches and Catholic properties around the city. The accords also established diplomatic relations between the Holy See and Italy. Catholicism was honored as the religion of the Italian state, and the church received financial awards, guarantees, and privileges. Clerical marriages, for example, were given equal status with civil ones, and diplomas from Catholic schools were accorded the same validity as those from state institutions. Another crucial concession was the state's recognition of the church-associated lay organizations, particularly Catholic Action and the Italian Catholic University Federation (*Federazione Universitaria Cattolica Italiana*, or FUCI), from which would come many of the nation's postwar leaders.

The Lateran Accords stand among Mussolini's greatest triumphs and evoked an enthusiastic response from the bulk of Italy's Catholic population, although some despaired that their pontiff would collaborate with the regime. The accords, however, enjoyed only the briefest of honeymoon periods and problems soon resurfaced in church–state relations. The Lateran Accords, however, ended the old Roman Question once and for all and presented Catholics the opportunity to reenter Italian public life after the disappointment of Don Sturzo's PPI and perhaps even dominate it if and when the Fascist regime expired.

Notes

1. Giorgio Candeloro, *Il movimento cattolico in Italia* (Rome: Riuniti, 1982), 387.
2. Denis Mack Smith, *Mussolini: A Biography* (New York: Random House, 1983), 27.
3. S. William Halperin, *Mussolini and Italian Fascism* (Princeton, N.J.: Van Nostrand, 1964), 29.
4. Norberto Bobbio, *Ideological Profile of Twentieth-Century Italy* (Princeton, N.J.: Princeton University Press, 1995), 128.
5. Claudio Segrè, *Italo Balbo: A Fascist Life* (Berkeley: University of California Press, 1987), 62–65.
6. Bobbio, *Ideological Profile*, 133.
7. Stanley G. Payne, *A History of Fascism, 1914–1945* (Madison: University of Wisconsin Press, 1995), 117.
8. Victoria de Grazia, *How Fascism Ruled Women: Italy, 1922–1945* (Berkeley: University of California Press, 1992), 158–59.
9. Halperin, *Mussolini and Italian Fascism*, 129.
10. Simonetta Falasca-Zamponi, *Fascist Spectacle: The Aesthetics of Power in Mussolini's Italy* (Berkeley: University of California Press, 2000), 100.

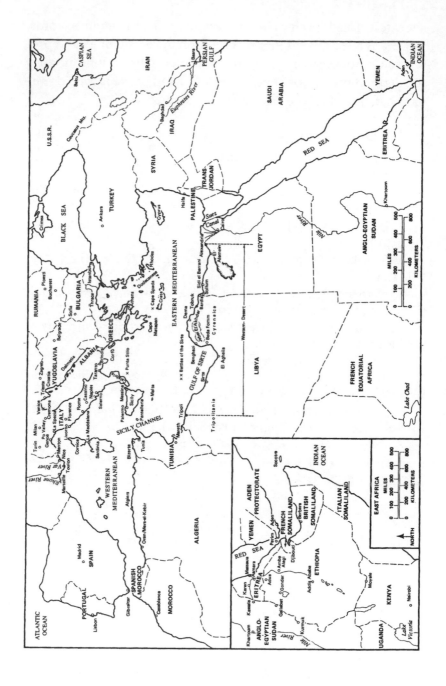

Chapter 3
Defeat and Liberation

O N THE EVENING OF MAY 9, 1936 Mussolini stepped from the Sala di Mappamondo, his colossal marbled office, onto the famous balcony over Rome's Piazza Venezia. He strutted into a scene to which the world had become accustomed. Above the adulatory roar of over one hundred thousand people assembled in the floodlit space below, the Duce proclaimed victory in the African war and the foundation of a new empire "on the fateful hills of Rome." On May 2, the defeated Negus, Emperor Haile Selassie, abandoned Addis Ababa to looters and boarded a train for the coast. Three days later, Marshal Pietro Badoglio, mounted on his white steed, restored order as he led a combined royal and blackshirt army into the vanquished capital. Pacification would take more time, but the war had ended and Italy had won it. Forgotten were Badoglio's role in the Caporetto disaster and his recommendations of martial law to stop the March on Rome in 1922. Now Mussolini honored him as the duke of Addis Ababa. As for King Victor Emmanuel, the Duce had hitched a suffix to his title. From 1936, he would be a king-emperor, just like the English monarchs.

The victory provided Mussolini with his greatest popularity. It was the final triumph in a seven-year epoch, however, that began with the Lateran Accords of 1929, an era in which Fascism reached as near as it ever would to a consensus among the Italian people, concord that would, nevertheless, very quickly prove flimsy. It was a time that hid or even buried much of the social tension that the Duce had created. In 1936, most seemed, nevertheless, to have fallen in line with the regime or had made their peace with it. The church did not challenge Mussolini's African adventure, and although Pope Pius XI privately criticized it, his public silence led some prelates such as Milan's cardinal Idelfonso Schuster to come very close to endorsing Italy's cause. The monarchy, the nobility, and the royalist armed forces complied with and contributed to the war effort. Business had been pulled or had pulled itself out of the worldwide depression. And the workers were docile. Mussolini's propaganda had pitted proletarian Italy against the plutocratic world, and its appeal to national unity worked. Resistance to the regime seemed unpatriotic.

But 1936 was not to be the beginning of Italian Fascism's golden age. Rather, it was the beginning of the end. The regime was running out of ideas and steam; its innovations of the middle and late 1920s were neither maturing nor bearing results. Part of the reason was the global economic crisis that began on Wall Street in 1929. The Depression did not affect Italy to the extent that it did the United States. Its 25 percent drop in exports, for example, paled against America's 64 percent. But Italy's depression was bad enough. From 1929 to 1933, the gross national product fell 5.4 percent, unemployment ballooned from three hundred thousand to one million, and many large concerns reached the brink of collapse.

The Duce responded not strictly within the framework of his Fascist corporate system, which froze in its tracks. Rather, he reacted with a form of state capitalism. Nevertheless, the idea of Rome coming to the rescue of tottering businesses fit easily into Mussolini's visions of the "ethical" superstate. His first such measure in November 1931 was to create the Istituto Mobiliare Italiano (IMI), an agency with the authority to bail out banks and companies through the issue of loans.

It was not enough, though, and the economic crisis deepened. So, in January 1933 Mussolini unveiled the more radical *Istituto per la Ricostruzione Industriale* (IRI). The IRI became a vast holding company, acquiring shares of failing firms; by 1936, it was Italy's chief source of industrial credit. By the start of World War II, the IRI controlled 44.15 percent of Italy's entire stock value and 17.8 percent of its capital. The IRI was not really Fascist, and it was not quite what the Duce had first envisioned. But it enabled the Italian state to claim a greater share of ownership of the economy than that found in any European nation outside the Soviet Union.

Meanwhile, however, the corporate state languished. The regime recognized its propaganda value and would always tout it as a key innovation of Mussolini's state. In 1939, for instance, the Chamber of Fasces and Corporations replaced the Chamber of Deputies. But the new body and the old one were both dead letters because decisions were made elsewhere. Corporatism had become little more than Fascist window dressing.

In the early 1930s, furthermore, Fascism's cause suffered the loss of many of Mussolini's most able lieutenants. In 1932, Dino Grandi left the Ministry of Foreign Affairs, the Ministry of Corporations lost Giuseppe Bottai, and the next year Italo Balbo left the Air Ministry. Grandi went to London as ambassador until he returned as minister of justice in 1939. Bottai turned to the social security (*previdenza sociale*) administration before becoming governor of Rome and, in 1936, returning to the cabinet as minister of national education. Jealous of Balbo's popularity, Mussolini pushed him out of the Air Ministry in 1933 to become governor of Libya, where he died in 1940.

Another loss occurred in December 1931 with the death of Arnaldo Mussolini, the Duce's brother. Arnaldo's worth rested in his closeness to Benito, possibly the Duce's only true male friend. The relationship bred an invaluable frankness now gone except perhaps for his wife and one or two of his mistresses, Margherita Sarfatti and, later, Claretta Petacci. With few now capable of telling him no and padded behind a wall of sycophants and corrupt officials, Mussolini embarked on a disastrous international policy of aggression, alliance with Nazi Germany, and war that would lead to catastrophe and ruin.

Arnaldo Mussolini could not be replaced, while the Duce, himself, succeeded Grandi at the Foreign Ministry, Bottai at Corporations, and Balbo at the Air Ministry. The worst figure to surface in the shake-up, also in December 1931, was Achille Starace. Disputes over treatment of the church had prompted the Duce to remove his capable party secretary, Giovanni Giurati, and supplant him with Starace. One of the very few southern Fascists of elevated rank, Starace was from Apulia, born in Gallipoli in 1889. He joined the movement in 1919 serving early on as a fence mender in party squabbles. As party secretary, Starace transformed the regime's attraction toward uniforms into a mania. He led silly campaigns to replace the handshake with the raised arm of the Roman salute and to substitute use of the "Lei" form of address, considered bourgeois and effete, with the more robust and Fascist "Voi." This new man was universally detested as a boorish cheerleader whose fawning praise embarrassed even the Duce, and he is perhaps best remembered for proving his Fascist virility by strutting around beaches and jumping through flaming hoops. The golden aura around Mussolini that Starace orchestrated, furthermore, only belittled the Duce's lieutenants. Propaganda still portrayed the *gerarchi* leadership as men of iron, but Starace's cult of Mussolini more and more dismissed them as lesser factotums.

The Nazi Challenge

The Fascist malaise was also linked inexorably to the fortunes of Adolf Hitler, who took office in Germany in 1933. The rise of Hitler signaled a deterioration of Mussolini's prestige. For over ten years after the March on Rome, Mussolini had enjoyed a certain status as dean of Europe's right-wing dictators, ahead of others such as Hungary's Miklos Horthy or Spain's Miguel Primo de Rivera. Unlike them, Mussolini's ambitions not just to rule his nation but to remake it elicited the genuine interest of intellectuals and observers around the globe. In the United States, business publications such as the *Wall Street Journal* and *Fortune* sang his praises as a man of action and a modernizer. As late as October 1938, pollsters queried Americans, "If you absolutely HAD to decide which dictator you liked best—Mussolini, Stalin [the Soviet dictator], or Hitler—which would you choose?" The Duce won handily with 53 percent, above Stalin's 34 and Hitler's 13.[1] Even the Broadway and film composer Cole Porter included Mussolini in the lyrics for his hit ditty "You're the Top!"

But Hitler and his upstart regime pushed Mussolini off center stage, and the Italian resented it. Germany was richer than Italy. There were more Germans than there were Italians. Germany's industry belched more smoke and churned out more destructive cannons than did Italy's. Mussolini had a big army, but Hitler had a bigger army. Mussolini bragged of eight million bayonets, of his air force blotting out the sun, of Fascism's manly toughness and of wars of aggression. But Hitler was more frightening.

Still, Mussolini's vanity was not the only reason for misgivings over Hitler. Geopolitical issues were at stake. Italy's trepidations of Germany may be reflected in the ambassadors chosen by Mussolini to represent Rome in Berlin through the 1930s. When the Führer came to power, Vittorio Cerruti was Italy's ambassador. Although he had acquired an early reputation as something of an eminence grise of the Nazi regime, Cerruti soon began to warn Rome of the Führer's ambitions in Austria and of the ugly anti-Semitism taking hold of Germany. By June 1935, therefore, it came as no surprise that Hitler obtained Cerruti's replacement. But the Fascists' next ambassador, Bernardo Attolico, held little sympathy for the Nazis and advocated the Pact of Steel mainly in the hope that an alliance with Germany would keep it in check. After the outbreak of war, Attolico's lack of enthusiasm prompted Hitler's intervention again, and another replacement arrived in April 1940. It was only at this late date that Mussolini dispatched to Berlin the notoriously pro-German propaganda boss, Dino Alfieri.

The omen of a greater Germany threatened Italy's ambitions in the Danube valley. Since shortly after the dissolution of the Hapsburg Empire in 1918, the Fascists had looked to the "rump" Austrian and Hungarian states as fertile terrain for some kind of arrangement under their leadership. In postwar Vienna and Budapest, right-wing or quasi-fascist regimes with revisionist foreign policies similar to Italy's had developed. Austria, furthermore, was strongly Catholic and shared a long border with Italy. In 1934, the new Austrian strongman was Engelbert Dollfuss. Initially cool to the Italians and more pro-French, he moved closer to Rome and even developed personal ties with Mussolini thanks to the intervention of Hungary's dictator, Julius Gömbös.

To protect his advantage and to keep a leash on Germany, in 1933 Mussolini proposed a "Four Power Pact" with Berlin, Paris, and London. The Duce had hoped the pact might flourish as an anti–League of Nations under his guidance. For their part, the British were frustrated by the breakdown of disarmament talks in 1932 and alarmed over Hitler's rise to power in January 1933, and they appeared open to Mussolini's idea of a new "Concert of Europe." On July 15, 1933, the pact was signed in Rome. But on October 14, Hitler walked out of the League, effectively rendering it a dead letter.

A year later, moreover, on July 25, 1934, Mussolini opposed Hitler without Franco–British support when Dollfuss was murdered in an attempted Nazi coup. On the day of his death, the Austrian leader's family was vacationing on the Adriatic shore with Mussolini, his wife, and children. They expected Dollfuss to arrive by plane later in the afternoon. When he heard of the murder, the enraged Duce sent troops to the Brenner Pass along the Austrian border. At a speech in Bari, he thundered against the Germans as "descendants of people who were totally illiterate in the days when Caesar, Virgil and Augustus flourished in Rome." The Fascist review, *Gerarchia*, furthermore, reminded Italians that the Austrians were a kindred "Roman, Mediterranean and Catholic" people. Hitler's plot failed, his threat to Austria passed, and Mussolini appeared to have won. But the Duce stood alone.

Any image of solidarity from the Four-Power Pact was a fiction. The Italians had been the only signatory to confront the Nazis.

International Tensions

The turning point in Italo–German relations came with the Ethiopian War. By the end of 1932, Mussolini decided to avenge the defeat of Adowa that Italy had suffered in 1896. Ethiopia would finally be absorbed into the Duce's twentieth-century Roman Empire. Early military plans for an invasion were entrusted to the old Quadrumvir, General Emilio De Bono, while diplomatic channels were piloted by Raffaele Guariglia. In March 1934, Mussolini published an alarmingly belligerent article, "*Verso il riarmo*," that denounced the League of Nations and indicated his intention to arm and conduct a quick war in Africa. By the autumn of that year, a sizeable Italian force had already passed through the Suez Canal on its way to the east African colonies of Eritrea and Somalia.

On December 5, 1934, Mussolini received his excuse for war at Wal Wal, an oasis in the middle of the Ogaden desert. Wal Wal was a "no man's land" in the empty wastes between Italian Somalia, British Somaliland, and Ethiopia. No power had ever really owned it, and only in 1929 did Addis Ababa begin to move toward it to consolidate its eastern frontier, a move that prompted an Anglo-Ethiopian commission to explore the area and find out exactly where the border was. Upon reaching Wal Wal, the commissioners were surprised to discover an Italian encampment already there. The British withdrew, leaving it to the Italians and Ethiopians, who opened up in an exchange of gunfire.

For Mussolini, Wal Wal would justify his invasion of Ethiopia, but diplomatic preparations also required attention. In January 1935, France's new foreign minister, Pierre Laval, traveled from Paris to Rome for meetings with the Duce. Their conversations led to an agreement wherein Italy surrendered its claims to Tunisia that had been based on the presence there of a large and well-established Italian community. In return, Rome felt that Paris acquiesced to its goals in east Africa. Laval's concession appears to have been little more than a silence or, at best, a wink, which Mussolini interpreted as the go-ahead. At the end of January, Great Britain's foreign secretary Sir John Simon promised Dino Grandi that he would keep Ethiopia off the League of Nations agenda. Like Laval's obscure signal, the Italians interpreted Simon's commitment as an endorsement.

Other British developments encouraged Mussolini further. The so-called Peace Ballot of June 1935 revealed most Britons did not consider places like Ethiopia worth fighting for. The Duce also obtained copies of London's secret "Maffey" report, which failed to locate any vital interests in Ethiopia and judged the Royal Navy as unprepared for a war in the Mediterranean. Consequently, Mussolini ignored some last-minute Anglo-French bluster at league headquarters in Geneva; on October 2, 1935, he gave the order for Italian troops to cross the border into Ethiopia. In a two-pronged invasion, the main force marched from Italy's colony of Eritrea while the other penetrated from Somalia.

In Geneva, the League of Nations branded Italy the aggressor and imposed sanctions on it for all products except oil. Negotiations started at once with France and Britain to lessen penalties and perhaps reach a settlement. The Franco-British desire to resolve conflicts with Mussolini and other dictators peacefully, even if it meant concessions, has forever been derided as "appeasement." One of the first examples of appeasement was the notorious Hoare–Laval Plan that was revealed in December 1935. Named for Pierre Laval and the new British foreign secretary, Sir Samuel Hoare, the proposal sacrificed slices of Ethiopia's territory to the Italians if the Duce would call a truce. Many observers labeled the Hoare–Laval plan as an outrageous submission to Fascist aggression. Worse, Mussolini took it as proof of Anglo-French weakness.

While the Hoare–Laval deal expired in humiliation and sanctions floundered, the regime delighted in an "us against the world" festival of patriotism. For the war chest, Queen Elena led married women to donate their gold wedding rings, while priests blessed replacements of less valuable metals. To show that Italians could go it alone despite the league's wish to starve them, patriots enjoyed bowls of "Sanctions Soup" made with home-grown, non-imported products. Confident of support among the people, Mussolini proceeded with his conquest.

The Ethiopian invasion in some ways resembled what Theodore Roosevelt termed America's "splendid little war" against Spain in 1898. Thirty-seven years later, the young journalist Indro Montanelli echoed the American president and dubbed Italy's campaign a "long and marvelous holiday." Blackshirt dignitaries poured into Africa to take a bite of the exotic campaign before it was all over. Two of Mussolini's sons, Vittorio and Bruno, served in air squadrons at the front. Vittorio compared his bombs exploding on Ethiopian cavalry to blooming roses although he confessed in his war memoir, *Flight over the Ambas*, that the effect was not quite as exciting as those explosions seen in American movies "when everything goes sky-high."[2] Party Secretary Starace led a mechanized unit into Gondar. One Fascist casualty was Roberto Farinacci who lost his right hand at a lake, fishing with grenades. Aristocrats went, too, led by the crown princess Maria José, who worked with the Red Cross.

The Fascist war machine proved capable of fulfilling its east African mission, but the task was not without some hitches. In the north, Emilio De Bono appeared unnecessarily timid and Rome replaced him with Pietro Badoglio. From the south, the more Fascist Rodolfo Graziani charged up the river valleys and through the Ogaden desert until bad weather slowed him down. In the air Italians employed up-to-date bombers against a nonexistent Ethiopian force. To speed the victory, moreover, the Italians polluted the African air with deadly mustard gas. The war's conclusive battle was fought in late March 1936 at Mai Chio, where Badoglio's army crushed and scattered the main Ethiopian force. The Negus escaped to Europe where he warned the League of Nations that his country would be only the first victim of Fascist aggression. In the end, 1,600 Italians surrendered their lives to give the Duce his African empire.

The war had strained Italy's relations with France and Britain. Their condemnations of the invasion, however, were offset by the hot and cold vacillations of appeasement and a reluctance to enforce sanctions. London's and Paris's postures irritated Mussolini, but their inaction left him unscathed. On the other hand, Germany and Italy followed a course that bound them closer. Hitler's regime supported Mussolini during the Ethiopian campaign and ignored the League's anti-Italian admonitions. High-level pronouncements of Italo–German solidarity, furthermore, were supported by unity of purpose at other ranks. For instance, meetings between the heads of German and Italian military intelligence, Admiral Wilhelm Canaris and General Mario Roatta in September 1935, and police bosses Heinrich Himmler and Arturo Bocchini the following April coordinated security forces in the fight against Bolshevism.

Rome's slide toward Berlin received a push in June 1936 when Mussolini selected the pro-German Galeazzo Ciano as foreign minister. Born in 1903, he was the son of one of the Duce's oldest allies, the Livornese admiral Costanzo Ciano. Rome had honored the father with title "Count of Cortellazzo" for daring wartime raids against the Austrians that he conducted along with his close friend, Gabriele d'Annunzio. In 1926, the Duce designated Count Ciano his successor as prime minister, should the occasion ever arise. Their alliance was cemented in 1930 when Galeazzo the son employed the status of his name, good looks, and a certain blackshirt ebullience to win the hand of Mussolini's daughter, Edda. In the Ethiopian War, he enhanced his promising diplomatic career by joining the "*Disperata*" bomber squadron. Returning to Italy in 1936, the Duce's Germanophile son-in-law found himself promoted to foreign minister. Soon after, on November 1, Mussolini announced that the world revolved on an axis that ran through Berlin and Rome. A year later, Italy joined Germany and Japan in an Anti-Comintern Pact directed at the Soviet Union. The doomed alliance was taking formal shape.

Austria was an early victim of this pro-German policy. Since the murder of Dollfuss, Mussolini had maintained a standing force at the Brenner Pass between Italy and Austria to safeguard against Nazi aggression. The new chancellor, Kurt Schuschnigg, remained loyal to Mussolini, and, at Geneva, Austria joined Albania and Hungary to support Italy against sanctions during the Ethiopian War. But the Italians withdrew some of their forces from the border during the war and Schuschnigg began to look for alternatives. Mussolini, too, had started to detach himself from Austria. Part of his scenario for Austrian defense included an anti-German partnership with France. But Paris's conduct after Dollfuss's death and its inability to block Hitler's occupation of the Rhineland in March 1936 convinced the Duce that the French could never deliver meaningful aid to Austria. Consequently, Mussolini encouraged Schuschnigg to live with the reality of his Nazi neighbor. When Germany chose to strike in March 1938, Mussolini assured Hitler that Italy no longer considered Austria a vital interest.

Military victory in Ethiopia and diplomatic defeat in the Danube basin pulled Italian foreign policy in a new direction, away from Europe, which had been abandoned to the Germans, and toward the Mediterranean. Mussolini had become a follower, not a leader, and his last major independent diplomatic initiative in Europe would be in the autumn of 1938 when he brought Germany, France, Britain, and Italy to the table at the Munich Conference. The meeting, however, only played into the Führer's hand, shamelessly awarding Czechoslovakia's Sudetenland to Hitler and merely delaying Berlin's absorption of the rest of the country until March 1939.

In keeping with Italy's Mediterranean orientation, between the fall of Addis Ababa and the start of World War II, Spain claimed most of Mussolini's ambitions. One of his few disappointments with his African adventure was the small number of Italians who had died in it. The war had not fulfilled one of Fascism's chief dreams, to toughen the Italians as a warrior race with great sacrifices of blood. General Francisco Franco's right-wing rebellion against the Spanish Republic, therefore, provided Rome with another opportunity to reach that goal. It would also help to circle

France with authoritarian powers and hasten the transition of the Mediterranean into a Fascist lake.

Mussolini had secretly supported right-wing causes against the Second Spanish Republic since its inception in 1931, but the start of the civil war on July 17, 1936, surprised him. Alarmed by news of German intervention plans and egged on by Ciano, the Duce dispatched men and equipment to aid Franco and his Nationalists against the Loyalist Republicans. Italian land forces constituted the Corpo di Truppe Volontarie, a "volunteer" force drawn from one Royal Army and three blackshirt divisions. Blackshirt troops were inspired by Fascist verve, although perhaps not enough to overcome their neglect of proper and up-to-date training. All told, about seventy-five thousand Italian soldiers served in Spain, and four thousand died there. Mussolini employed other services as well in the battle against the Spanish republic. Military intelligence, for example, served its purpose in the war and unmarked Italian submarines and other craft preyed on and sank 78,800 tons of shipping headed for Republican ports.

With so much assistance to Franco, meddlesome Italian advisers felt they had paid for the right to tell the Spanish *Caudillo* how to run the war. But Franco favored a slow campaign and resented the demands of his obtrusive allies for a quick victory in typical Fascist style. He did not, therefore, share Italy's embarrassment that came from defeat at Guadalajara in March 1937. There, fresh from the conquest of Malaga, the troops of General Mario Roatta were caught in a muddy ravine and suffered a humiliation at the hands of enemy forces, many of whom were anti-Fascist Italian exiles. Here was a defeat that Franco could accept. The debacle had not been catastrophic for the *Caudillo* and had shamed his Italian allies just enough to give him a leg up against them.

In January 1939, Franco took Barcelona with Italian help and soon overran the rest of the Republican stronghold of Catalonia. Madrid and Valencia, the last holdouts, surrendered in March, and the Spanish civil war drew to a close. Mussolini and his allies had won. But the euphoria of Ethiopia was not to be repeated. The war had not been popular at home, and Italy had grown ever more estranged from France and Britain.

Forging an alliance with Hitler, however, continued apace. In September 1937, Mussolini affirmed the pro-Berlin direction of Italian foreign policy by visiting Germany. There, military reviews awed and convinced the Duce of Nazi invincibility, while mass demonstrations of adoring German crowds flattered him. For someone who had himself choreographed "spontaneous" mass exhibitions, such displays showed Mussolini to be surprisingly gullible. While privately, Mussolini still ridiculed his German partner, the public Duce undertook embarrassing public measures to prove his commitment to the Nazis, such as adopting the German goose step for the Italian army.

In 1938, the darkest manifestation of this pro-German policy came in decrees directed at Italy's forty-five thousand Jews. Mussolini's positions on the Jews and on other racial matters had been ambiguous until the mid-1930s. In the past, he rejected racist thinking and acknowledged Jewish contributions to his regime. But the conquest of Ethiopia forced Italy to deal with large numbers of nonwhites in its empire and accelerated the drive toward bigotry that had always lurked beneath Fascist (and Italian) imperialism. Warmer relations with the Nazis brought the question to the top of the agenda, and Mussolini complied, telling the Germans anything that he felt they wanted to hear. In July 1938, he published his "Race Charter" that branded Arabs, black Africans, and Jews as inferior peoples. Measures followed to exclude Jews from public employment and the universities.

The Duce's persecution would never approximate the nightmare of the Führer's. Yet, as Mussolini's biographer Denis Mack Smith wrote, "the man who ordered prisoners of war to be executed, and the gassing of whole villages in Libya and Ethiopia, who was so sorry that so few Italians had been killed in east Africa and who, according to Ciano, would not think twice before firing on a crowd of hunger demonstrators, was not a man to stop short if he thought Hitler wished him to expel the Jews from Italy."[3]

Victory in Spain and the suspicion that he was slipping behind Nazi Germany whetted the Duce's appetite for more foreign glory. He resisted the temptation to relax after Spain and take stock of the nation's readiness for another conflict. If he had surrendered to it, he would have discovered the bankrupt state and exhaustion of his armed forces. Instead, he quickly relaunched his belligerent policy toward other corners of the Mediterranean.

Seemingly oblivious to the dangerous world of 1939, Mussolini felt that one more morsel could be digested: rugged and impoverished Albania. Although the Treaty of Tirana in 1926 already secured the country as an Italian protectorate, Albania looked like an easy victory that would uphold Fascist Italy's prestige as a warrior nation. The Duce had been initially reluctant to annex Albania because of his occupations with Spain and for fear of upsetting cordial relations with Yugoslavia's prime minister, Milan Stojadinovic. Rather, his son-in-law, Count Ciano, first championed the idea of a strike against Albania in 1937. But the coming resolution of the Spanish war, German aggression in Czechoslovakia, the resignation of Stojadinovic, and rumors of intrigues in Croatia prompted Mussolini to come around to Ciano's opinion. Despite abysmal planning and near chaos among the military chiefs in Rome, Albania's fate was sealed.

On Good Friday, April 7, 1939, the Duce's soldiers landed on Albania's coast. They were commanded by Alfredo Guzzoni, one of his better generals, and met with only minimal resistance. King Zogu and his Hungarian wife, who had just given birth to their son, promptly fled, and the Italians annexed the country after a few days. Although Victor Emmanuel considered the conquest a waste of time, he deigned to accept "king of Albania" as one of his titles.

One month later, on May 6, Ciano met Germany's foreign minister, Joachim Ribbentrop, in Milan. Although both nations were moving toward a formal alliance, the meeting had no clear agenda. News, however, reached Mussolini in Rome that the Milanesi had given the German an icy reception and, even worse, French papers reported that the Italians had jeered Hitler's envoy.

On the evening of May 6, the fuming Duce telephoned Ciano and ordered him to sign an alliance with Germany. Hitler agreed through Ribbentrop, and events moved quickly. A German draft for an aggressive alliance was approved by the Italians, and the Pact of Steel was a signed document by May 22.

The new alliance, however, could not erase the fact that the two dictators never coordinated their plans for conquest and domination. Mussolini envisioned the ultimate struggle beginning sometime after 1942, a date with nothing in common with Hitler's accelerating march to war in 1939. Without consulting his Italian ally, Hitler resolved to attack Poland. He recognized, however, that this required the unthinkable: an agreement with Stalin, the Bolshevik devil in Moscow. Despite the ups and downs in German-Italian relations, the one vision that had always united them portrayed the Soviet regime as the abominable heart of evil. Their Anti-Comintern Pact against the Soviet Union, furthermore, was still in force. Consequently, when Hitler unveiled his Polish intentions to Ciano on August 11–12 and announced the Nazi–Soviet Non-Aggression Pact on August 23, he shocked the Italians. Stung particularly hard was the betrayed foreign minister, whose faith in a German alliance shook to its core.

Rome could only respond that without enormous amounts of aid, purposefully unreasonable amounts, it could not join Germany in the impending adventure. But Hitler did not need Italy to invade Poland and respectfully declined to fill Mussolini's grocery list. On September 1, German troops crossed the border on their way to Warsaw. World War II had begun while the Duce sat on the sidelines, frustrated and embarrassed.

Mussolini had to face the ugly little secret that his warrior nation was completely unprepared for any conflict. Italy's economy was still largely based in agriculture, and its industrial levels sat far below those of the other Western powers. The African and Spanish wars had severely strained Italy's meager resources; and Fascism's long hold on power assured the development of endemic corruption in the military. Mussolini's undersecretary in the War Ministry and army chief of staff, General Alberto Pariani, was one example—a gross incompetent who misled the Duce about Italy's miserable situation. Consequently, an enormous gap separated the real figure of Italy's war resources with that of what Mussolini believed them to be. His projected strength of 1,700,000 men under arms, for instance, was a preposterous exaggeration. The trusted general Guzzoni reported that only ten of Italy's sixty-seven divisions were ready for action.

The air force was in an even more precarious position, a dilemma revealed in September 1939 when the official entrusted to coordinate war preparations, Carlo Favagrossa, requested a detailed account of the service's resources. General Giuseppe Valle, the bellicose undersecretary since 1929, simply refused Favagrossa. As it turned out, Valle's brag of over two thousand planes was more than twice the real figure of 841 bombers and fighters, 240 of which were under repair.[4] In October, the Duce fired both Pariani and Valle. He reorganized his cabinet as well and dismissed Achille Starace as party secretary. But the damage had already been done.

The reduced armaments figures strapped and humbled Mussolini. But hubris got the better of him and, rather than look like a mere neutral, he proclaimed Italy's status as a "nonbelligerent" at the side of Germany. Privately, the Duce's commitment to Germany was more ambivalent. To some he declared his intent to fight a "parallel war," sooner or later, next to Hitler. Still, like the moth at the flame, his opinions in the first months of the war swung back and forth from pro-German to anti-German and back again. Ciano was encouraged on those days when the Duce ranted against the Nazi alliance. As 1939 turned into 1940, the two must have experienced some glee when Italy sent aid to Finland, which fought its defensive "winter war" against Hitler's new ally, the Soviet Union.

Mussolini searched for a way out through the end of the year and into 1940. The Nazis had not yet unleashed their Blitzkrieg (lightning war) against the West, and the Duce hoped to bring the sides together as he had done at Munich in 1938. But Hitler dismissed those feelers, and on April 9, the Blitzkrieg exploded on the West with invasions of Denmark and Norway. In May, the German onslaught swept through the Low Countries and imperiled France. On the 29th, an anxious Mussolini conceded to Pietro Badoglio that Hitler had won the war and that Italy needed to strike somewhere, anywhere, to partake of the spoils. Badoglio and others reported that the Duce more than once made the cynical claim that only a few thousand dead would guarantee Italy a place at the peace table.

On June 10, therefore, a hungry Mussolini finally declared war on Britain and France. But his proclamation failed to instill fears of an unstoppable Fascist juggernaut. Rather, the circumstances of its timing made Italy appear as a cowardly opportunist against a prostrate France. The hand that held the dagger, Franklin Roosevelt announced, had plunged it into the back of its neighbor. Considering Italy's inability to fight, Mussolini's declaration of war was as much an irresponsible act of folly as it was a tragedy. "I am sad, very sad," wrote Ciano in his diary. "The adventure begins. May God help Italy!"[5]

The War

Italy celebrated few military victories in World War II, the record of which was marked by one defeat after the other. The first disaster was the invasion of France, directed in the field by Crown Prince Umberto. Unsure of risking his troops at what was apparently the end of the fight, from Rome Mussolini directed the prince to maintain defensive positions until he realized the war was, indeed, over. Only on June 20, after Paris requested an armistice, did Umberto launch an advance of a few paltry and embarrassing miles.

France fell, but instead of an iron-willed march of conquest, Fascist Italy's contribution to the campaign was a shameful blot. Anxious to repair the damage, to appear as a full equal in the Axis alliance and to prove Italy's mettle elsewhere, Mussolini touted his "parallel war" alongside the Nazis. As the Mediterranean power,

Italy would take care of the Balkans, and on October 28, its troops crossed the Albanian border into Greece. But Athens delivered such stiff resistance that it repelled the invaders back into Albania, and Mussolini's commander, General Ubaldo Soddu, advised him to seek an armistice. Instead, on January 19–20, 1941, the humiliated Duce went hat in hand to Germany. His parallel war had failed, and Hitler's help had become indispensable. But now the Germans had their price. The Führer harangued Mussolini for two hours, outlining his plans for the Mediterranean and for Italy's subordinate place in those plans. In the spring the Führer fulfilled his part of the bargain. His and the Duce's troops trampled both Yugoslav and Greek independence, and the Adriatic became an Italian lake. But Rome had become the junior partner in the Axis.

At sea, the navy fared no better. On the night of November 11–12, 1940, a force of British "Swordfish" torpedo bombers attacked the fleet in Taranto harbor and sent three battleships to the bottom. The following March 28, the British, aided by radar and a knowledge of the Italian code, surprised a large force off Cape Matapan in Greece and sank three heavy cruisers. In both exchanges, the British lost not a single ship. Still, successful sabotage raids by Italian frogmen combined with the demands of the Pacific war to reduce British naval strength in the Mediterranean. But oil shortages and timid commanders saw to it that the Italian fleet would stay in port as much as possible.

In the colonies, the British easily chased the Italians out of east Africa. They crossed into Ethiopia on January 18, 1941, and the last of Mussolini's forces there surrendered on the following November 18. Haile Selassie reclaimed his throne, while Italy's last viceroy, Amedeo Umberto, the duke of Aosta, died of tuberculosis in a Kenyan prisoner-of-war camp.

In north Africa, Italian plans to dominate the Mediterranean hinged on Libya, and from there Marshal Graziani launched an ill-prepared invasion of Egypt. Desperately short of transport, the advance fizzled, and the Italians sat for months in a string of desert camps. In December 1940, the British retaliated with an offensive that pushed the Italians back into Libya. By the beginning of February 1941, the British had taken 115,000 Italian prisoners, and Graziani had resigned. Again the Italians turned to the Germans, relinquishing control of their north African campaign to Irwin Rommel, the "Desert Fox," who arrived in Libya on February 11, 1941.

Rommel was another embarrassment for Mussolini although his command did not save north Africa. The final act there began in October 1942 when Britain's field marshal Bernard Montgomery's victory at El Alamein started the total sweep of the Italo–German forces from Egypt and Libya. In November, furthermore, America's general Dwight Eisenhower launched "Operation Torch," the invasion of French North Africa (America had been Britain's ally since December 1941). His bases secured in Morocco and Algeria, he then directed the Allied march eastward to link with Montgomery's Commonwealth forces. By the spring of 1943, the two prongs of this pincer closed in Tunisia, where German and Italian resistance collapsed.

Rommel failed to produce miracles in Libya, and suddenly the Germans appeared less invincible than before. At the same time, the war on the Eastern Front turned against the Nazis. When Hitler declared war on the Soviet Union in June 1941, Mussolini followed suit and sent a quarter of a million soldiers there. In January 1943, however, the Axis suffered their titanic defeat at Stalingrad, and the collapse of Hitler's empire had begun.

At home, discontent spread. The Allies intensified their aerial bombardments of Italy's industrial north in the autumn of 1942, and the hardships of war pushed factory workers there to launch massive strikes in early 1943. Exiled anti-Fascists, moreover, were heartened by a clandestine opposition that fed and grew on the discontent. By 1943, underground Communist, Socialist, and Catholic organizations had formed and were joined by the Action Party, a new group of progressive republicans and liberals that formed in January 1943 from the Justice and Liberty movement of the Rosselli brothers, Carlo and Nello, whom the Fascists had murdered in France in 1937.

At higher levels, industrialists secretly renewed old ties with Anglo-American colleagues. The Catholic Church also moved to disassociate itself with the regime. With the possible exception of patriotic impulses that brought together church and state during the Ethiopian War, relations between Mussolini's regime and the Holy See had deteriorated through the 1930s and into the war years. Eugenio Pacelli, a Roman who became Pope Pius XII in 1939, angered Mussolini by exchanging visits with the king and by not suppressing uncensored war bulletins. In April 1940, Roberto Farinacci even fumed that the Vatican daily, *L'osservatore romano*, had become a Jewish mouthpiece. The Royal House was another faction displeased with the regime. The king instructed his household minister, the Duke of Acquarone, to discuss with military leaders the possibility of replacing Mussolini, a conspiracy that would include pre-Fascist leaders, aristocrats, and even some disgruntled *gerarchi*.

Events at the front, however, forced the issue. The Allies followed their north African victory with the invasion of Italy. On June 11, they took the tiny Mediterranean island of Pantelleria, a rock fortified with great fanfare in the 1930s but that now proved useless. It was the first bit of Italian home territory to fall.

The Fall of Mussolini

"Operation Husky," the Allied invasion of Sicily, was implemented on the night of July 9–10, 1943, with landings of 160,000 men along the island's southern coast. General Guzzoni, who had led the invasion of Albania, was entrusted with Sicily's defense. One of the few to predict the landings correctly, Guzzoni's pleas for mobile armored units fell on deaf ears in Rome, and Fascist resistance on Sicily crumbled within weeks. Palermo surrendered on July 24, and fighting largely ceased with the fall of Messina on August 18.

The shock of Allied beachheads in Sicily was repeated on July 19 when the Allies bombed Rome from the air. The capital had been mostly spared throughout the war; but now the Anglo-Americans wanted to send the Italian government a clear message. Many of the shells were designated for the Termini railroad station but went astray and hit the adjacent working class San Lorenzo quarter, killing 1,500 people. News of the attack reached Mussolini during a meeting with Hitler in the north Italian town of Feltre, a conference at which, many hoped, the Duce would confront the Führer and announce Italy's withdrawal from the war. Instead, the sullen dictator, physically ill and very tired, sat and bobbed his head while Hitler harangued on and on about the Judeo–Bolshevik conspiracy. The Duce lacked the nerve after all, incapable of steering Italy from its rocky fate. After the meeting, Mussolini's disgusted chief of the general staff, Vittorio Ambrosio, submitted his resignation.

Back in Rome, King Victor Emmanuel's personal inspection of the damaged San Lorenzo neighborhood was met with catcalls and insults from the crowd. The shaken monarch resolved that the time had come to cut the Duce's power once and for all and pull Italy from the war. The mechanics of the coup had been in the works for some time, planned by a Carabinieri general, Azolino Hazon. But Hazon was killed in the July 19 bombardment, and the task went to Angelo Cerica.

The bell tolled for Mussolini at an all-night meeting of the Grand Council of Fascism on July 24–25, 1943. In the past, the Grand Council had served as a limited exchange of ideas and as a rubber stamp for the Duce. It had not met at all since 1939, but now Italy's extraordinary circumstances gave it a new importance. The evening's discussion turned into angry debate on a motion from Dino Grandi that the Italian state reassume its duties from the Fascist Party and that Mussolini surrender his powers to the king. Grandi expected the worst and recorded that as he argued his case, he kept two hand grenades in his briefcase. But Grandi needed no bombs. For whatever reason, Mussolini chose not to fight.

In the end, Grandi's motion passed nineteen to seven. Even Ciano sided against his father-in-law. Roberto Farinacci voted separately on his own resolution. The afternoon after the Grand Council decision, Mussolini appeared at the Villa Savoia, where Victor Emmanuel informed him that the war had been lost and that he had designated Marshal Pietro Badoglio as Italy's next prime minister.

On his way out the Duce met a troop of Carabinieri police who took him into custody without incident. Word spread quickly, and jubilant throngs took to the streets to exalt Badoglio, the king, the end of the war and the rebirth of Italian democracy. Hopes of peace and freedom electrified Italy. After the Grand Council meeting, crowds of people armed with hammers and chisels rid government buildings of the stone fasces that had adorned them while images of the king, and Badoglio quickly emerged in streets and piazzas.

The ease with which Mussolini's dictatorship collapsed revealed that, after three years of defeat and humiliation, support for the regime had sunk to abysmal levels. With the Duce removed, most of the edifice that he had constructed for over twenty years seemed to vanish overnight. The Fascist Party was dissolved and so many *gerarchi* had disappeared that Marshal Badoglio waited a month before he opted to arrest the few important ones that remained. His decision, moreover, resulted from a fear that the blackshirts might facilitate some kind of German retaliation. Whole organizations like the Militia, the Balilla, and the Fasci Feminili disappeared in an instant, while others, such as Dopolavoro, the workers' leisure agency, limped into the postwar world often under new names.

But that path was Italy to take? During the month and a half that followed Mussolini's fall, Badoglio's government, dubbed the "45 Days," existed in a limbo between war and peace, between truth and falsehoods. Italy's stomach to fight was long gone, if it had ever existed at all; but the marshal announced that the nation would continue the war at Germany's side. At the same time, he opened secret negotiations with the Allies.

The "Catastrophe"

The ambiguity was resolved in Italy's national catastrophe of the night of September 8–9. Badoglio's aim to pull the nation out of the war had been clear to the Germans from the start, and they had prepared for the betrayal by pouring troops down the peninsula and securing strategic places as they went. In the Reich's view, such precautions were sound. Badoglio's peace feelers led to secret negotiations in Sicily between the Allied forces under the command of General Eisenhower and Italy's general Giuseppe Castellano. On September 3, the Allies effected a preliminary beachhead in Calabria, and a secret "short" armistice, covering military matters, was signed at Cassibile, near Syracuse.

But disaster loomed in the inability of either side to trust the other. Two days after the Cassibile signatures, Major Luigi Marchesi of Castellano's staff returned to Rome with vague information that the major invasion of the mainland would come sometime between September 10 and 15. He did not know that the Anglo-Americans targeted September 9 to announce the armistice and coordinate it with a seaborne landing in Salerno and an airborne one in Rome. Allied reluctance to be completely open in their military plans frustrated Badoglio and the prime minister's reticence angered Eisenhower. Reports that Germany had secured Rome's airfields worried the Supreme Commander and he clandestinely sent a representative, General Maxwell Taylor, there to see for himself and discuss the situation with the Italians. Yet the American was denied access to the prime minister and was disappointed by the lack of commitment he discerned from Badoglio's underlings. On the evening of September 8, therefore, and against the pleas of Badoglio, Eisenhower went ahead and announced the armistice. The Salerno invasion was launched, but the Rome-bound planes, under General Taylor's command, were called back as they sat on the runways.

Eisenhower was not the only figure who left Rome to its fate. Italy's leaders did as well. Instead of standing with their forces to defend the capital from the Germans, Badoglio and King Victor Emmanuel forgot their duty and fled to the south. Under cover of night their motorcade left the city and drove east toward the port of Ortona. From there, a navy corvette, the *Baionetta*, transported them down the Adriatic coast to Brindisi, which they hoped would be in Allied hands the next morning.

The king and Badoglio had left Italy's armed forces completely in the dark. Only a brief radio message at 7:45 P.M. from the prime minister announced that the Allies had granted an armistice, that the troops were not to resist the Anglo-Americans and that they should "react to eventual attacks from any other quarter." In other words, Italy's soldiers were on their own. Badoglio had even neglected to inform his cabinet of his escape plan.

From Sicily, Eisenhower urged the king and Badoglio to "issue immediately a clarion call to all patriotic Italians [to] seize every German by the throat." But the American plea fell on silence and the collapse of Italy had begun. Allied forces took control of the south, while the Germans secured the north.

Across the peninsula, leaderless forces reacted haphazardly as each situation warranted. In the south, most submitted promptly to the Allies. Much different was the north where hundreds of thousands of Italian soldiers were disarmed by their former allies and sent to work camps in Germany. Many complied and surrendered, or they abandoned their posts for home. In Rome, some units put up a stiff but futile resistance against the Germans, particularly near the Porta San Paolo. Closer to the Salerno beachhead, Naples experienced a mass revolt that ended when the Germans abandoned the city on September 30.

Much of Italy's forces stationed in Yugoslavia joined the anti-German partisan fighters. Soldiers in Greece outnumbered their German counterparts although the latter operated with more and better equipment. The island of Cephalonia, off Greece's western shore, provided one the most unforgettable illustrations of the chaos. Of its 12,000-man Italian garrison, 1,250 died in combat defending the island from the Germans, who murdered 5,000 more after their surrender. Another roughly 4,000 died when the three ships transporting them to the mainland hit mines and sank. About 1,200 who escaped before the slaughter joined Greek resistance forces against the Nazis.

The Germans and the North

After September 8, some blackshirts appeared behind German lines to offer their services and construct a neo-Fascist state. But

Berlin still wanted the Duce to head it and dispatched a rescue squad to free him from confinement atop one of Italy's highest mountains, the Gran Sasso d'Italia in Abruzzo. On September 12, Otto Skorzeny led a German commando raid at the ski resort where Mussolini was kept and liberated him without a shot. The deposed blackshirt was escorted to Hitler's headquarters on the Russian front where, over the radio, he reluctantly announced his return to head a resurrected Fascist state. By the end of the month, the Germans arranged for the Duce to head a collaborationist regime in northern Italy, known ultimately as the Italian Social Republic (*Repubblica Sociale Italiana*, or RSI). Administration centers were scattered across the north, from Milan to Brescia to Venice. The regime's unofficial name, the Salò Republic, in fact, derived from a small resort town on Lake Garda's western shore at which the Ministry of Popular Culture and the Press Office were located. Mussolini spent most of his final days near Salò at the Villa Feltrinelli.

The RSI was thus born as a shadow, or perhaps a ghost, of Mussolini's earlier regime. Neither he nor any other Italian Fascist wielded any authentic power, a powerlessness reflected in the Duce's schedule, which consisted largely of writing newspaper columns or strolling through the villa gardens, a routine that afforded him considerable rest, and his health made a substantial improvement.

Few of the old faces surfaced in the Salò government. With German help, the Fascists arrested some of the July 25 conspirators and put them on trial. They shot most of the defendants, including the old Quadrumvir Emilio De Bono and Mussolini's son-in-law, Ciano. Among the other *gerarchi*, Grandi and Bottai had fled Italy. Farinacci and Starace joined the Duce in the north but assumed no commands there, relics of a lost crusade. Marshal Rodolfo Graziani led what little existed of the RSI's army, and the philosopher Giovanni Gentile continued to serve the cause until 1944 when anti-Fascist partisans ambushed him in Florence and shot him.

In this blackshirt vacuum, leadership often fell to a new group that included such figures as Party Secretary Alessandro Pavolini, who had joined the Fascists in 1920 and worked in the Florence machine, but became the minister of popular culture only in 1939; and Vittorio Mussolini, the Duce's son who acted as a behind-the-scenes power broker. The real masters of Italy, however, were the Germans: Field Marshal Albert Kesselring at the front, and two Nazi envoys to Salò, Ambassador Rudolf von Rahn and SS general Karl Wolff.

The Reich, furthermore, served itself to some Italian territory. Along the former Austrian border, Germany combined the old Hapsburg lands in the Trentino and Alto Adige with the province of Belluno and annexed it as *Alpenvorland*. It also absorbed Istria and other parts of the eastern border as *Adriatisches Kustenland*, ruled by a *gauleiter* in Trieste. Mussolini's apparatus to Italianize those areas during the 1930s was quietly dismantled, and the areas' German qualities were henceforth groomed.

A November 1943 Fascist congress at Verona drafted a new constitution that flirted with many of the old leftist ideas dormant since the 1919 San Sepolcro platform. The Duce, for example, activated plans for workers' participation in industrial management and decisions. When the reforms were introduced in 1944, however, they only interested Fascist stalwarts. The plan annoyed corporate management and the Germans, while most of the workers considered it a ruse and refused to cooperate. But such questions were moot since the real purpose for the RSI was not to launch social experiments but rather to aid Germany's war effort.

Still, only on rare occasions did RSI troops participate in combat at the front. Mussolini's army had either been conscripted in labor projects in Germany or assigned the sad and demoralizing task of waging war on fellow Italians—deserters and opponents of the regime. To meet this charge, the Duce's regular troops were reinforced by criminal gangs in black shirts that terrorized the population, private armies of sadists and murderers known as the "Black Brigades."

Subservience to the Reich also meant new compliance with German orders for roundups of Jews. The Holocaust had come to Italy. On September 26, Herbert Kappler, Rome's SS commander,

demanded fifty kilograms of gold to spare the city's Jewish population. Pope Pius XII offered to cover whatever the Jews, themselves, could not raise, although the offer was not needed and the
precious metal was delivered as ordered. But the duplicitous Kappler reneged on his word, and on the night of October 16, 1943,
the SS descended on Rome's Jewish quarter. Roundups followed
in other Italian cities over the next few months, and, all told,
about 7,500 Jews were sent to the Reich's death camps. Most never
returned.

The bulk of Italy's Jewish population, however, did not suffer
extermination. With Denmark, Italy shares the honor of Western
Europe's highest survival rate in the Holocaust, testament in large
part to a culture that resisted Nazi intentions. Certainly some Fascist die-hard racists such as Giovanni Preziosi endorsed Hitler's
reign of terror. But Jews were secretly harbored throughout Italy
by all manner of Italians, in private homes, monasteries, and
churches. About 450 were accorded shelter in the Vatican itself.

The Allies and the South

While the Germans controlled northern Italy, a different situation
existed in the south that was dominated by the Allies. The job of liberation rested mainly in two large armies, the Fifth U.S. and the
British Eighth. Along with contingents from the Commonwealth,
the French Empire, Poland, Brazil, and other nations, they were
eventually placed under the overall command of Field Marshal Sir
Harold Alexander. South of the front, at Brindisi, the king and
Badoglio consolidated their rule in an arrangement popularly
known as the "Kingdom of the South" (*Regno del Sud*). This
makeshift state followed the Allies north, moving first to Salerno
and finally Rome in June 1944. It dutifully declared war on Germany on October 13, 1943, but never achieved full allied status with
Britain and America. Rather, as Britain's Prime Minister Churchill
stated, Italy needed to "work her passage" as a "cobelligerent," a
sting that recalled Mussolini's "nonbelligerent" idea of 1939.

The kingdom was hardly independent, and most important decisions emanated from Allied headquarters at the royal palace at Caserta outside Naples. At the front, draconian military government ruled, but the Anglo-Americans were anxious to hand over as much as possible of liberated Italy to the Italians themselves. To keep an eye on them, however, an Allied Control Commission (renamed "Allied Commission" [AC] in September 1944) maintained a supervisory role with veto power over the Kingdom of the South. For much of the period, the head of the AC was Harold Macmillan of the British publishing house. And it was he who possessed final word over Italy's day-to-day administration.

The Allies, particularly the Americans, permitted and encouraged the rebirth of free politics to ensure that Italy not revert back to some kind of authoritarianism under Victor Emmanuel and Badoglio. This goal required that active and independent parties be allowed to operate in post-Fascist Italy. They had briefly surfaced during the 45 Days but were quickly driven back underground when the Nazis occupied Rome. There, in December 1943, the subterranean opposition formed a coalition, the Committee of National Liberation (*Comitato di Liberazione Nazionale*, or CLN). Chaired by the pre-Fascist prime minister, Ivanoe Bonomi, the CLN ultimately included representatives of the Christian Democrats, Socialists, Communists, Liberals, Bonomi's tiny faction of Labor Democrats, and the Action Party.

The CLN held its first public congress at liberated Bari in January 1944. The Bari meeting illustrated the chasm that now separated the CLN from the Kingdom of the South. From all quarters came blistering demands for the king's abdication and surrender of the reins of government to the coalition. The Allies recognized that the CLN had captured the initiative over the king and Badoglio and had become the real voice of liberated Italy. Its ascent to power was only a matter of time.

Much but not quite all of the CLN Bari program was fulfilled in the next few months. Victor Emmanuel stubbornly refused to abdicate. But he finally compromised with the Allies when the Neapolitan jurist Enrico De Nicola and the Liberal philosopher

Benedetto Croce convinced him that he had no choice. The king was permitted to retain his title, but upon the liberation of Rome his royal responsibilities would be transferred to Crown Prince Umberto, who would assumed the title "Lieutenant General of the Realm." On June 4, 1944, units of the American Fifth Army under General Mark Clark entered the capital. Within days, Badoglio resigned and a CLN government under Prime Minister Bonomi took power. Winston Churchill fumed against the "ambitious wind bags" and the "aged and hungry politicians," but the Allied Commission acquiesced to the new situation.

Churchill had little reason to worry; Bonomi's cabinet was a coalition led by moderates who promised not to rock the boat. It may have been an anti-Fascist government, but it was not a revolutionary one. The key to CLN stability was its Communist representative Palmiro Togliatti. In March, he had returned to Italy from the Soviet Union and announced full cooperation with Badoglio. Togliatti had even joined the cabinet in April as minister without portfolio and continued in that role under Bonomi. The revolution was defused at least as far as the Communists were concerned. But a wild card remained in Pietro Nenni, the fiery Socialist who saw opportunities for Marxist gains. As a CLN leader, Nenni found a place in Bonomi's first ministry. But when the prime minister reshuffled his cabinet in December 1944 after a crisis over purging Fascists, Nenni lost his seat and, the following spring, even served briefly in prison for an inflammatory speech.

Resistance and Liberation

Bonomi's most difficult task was to control or tame the radical resistance that had emerged against the Fascists in the German-occupied north. There, the Committee of National Liberation for Upper [*Alta*] Italy (*Comitato di Liberazione Nazionale Alt'Italia*, or CLNAI) was headquartered in Milan and sanctioned by Rome. The CLNAI agreed to follow Allied directives, submit to a commander from Rome, Raffaele Cadorna, and lay down its arms at the end of the war. The northern coalition was composed of the same parties found in Rome's CLN with the exception of Bonomi's Labor Democrats, but the resistance rank and file leaned much more profoundly to the political Left than did their cousins in the south. Cadorna, for instance, was largely a figure head compared to his vice commanders, the Communist Luigi Longo and the Action Party's Ferruccio Parri. Much of the resistance's avant-garde, furthermore, was composed of Communist-dominated Gruppi d'Azione Pattriotica (GAP) fighters and Squadre di Azione Patriottica (SAP) workers engaged in sabotage.

As the Anglo-American armies inched northward toward victory, the resistance ranks swelled. The Allies kept track of the rise and estimated that between fifteen and twenty thousand Italians had taken up arms in the fall of 1943. By the end of January 1944, the number had risen to 42,000 and then 109,000 by the following July. The region of Piedmont, particularly its hills and mountains, contained the highest concentration of fighters, between forty and fifty thousand, followed by the Veneto with twenty to thirty thousand, Lombardy with twenty thousand, and Emilia with about ten thousand.[6] By the war's end, about 250,000 Italians called themselves partisans, claims that smacked of the "sunshine soldier" and warranted some degree of skepticism.

The resistance forces rarely tangled head-on in pitched battles with the Nazis and Fascists. Their purpose, rather, was to harass the enemy in hit-and-run raids from bases in the countryside or to sabotage factory production, communications, and transportation. Travel between towns became more and more difficult, and the cities turned into armed Fascist camps. The situation fueled in part Salò's enormous black market economy, which prized hard-to-get farm bounties.

Salò and German forces unleashed vicious and merciless reprisals against both partisans and innocent hostages during the last year and a half of the war. When a partisan bomb, for instance, killed 33 German troops in Rome's via Rasella (soldiers from the ex-Italian Alpenvorland), the Nazis retaliated with the murder of 335 people and sealed their bodies in the Ardeatine caves outside the city. The worst massacre occurred at the end of September and the beginning of October 1944 near Bologna. There, the Germans destroyed the village of Marzabotto and slaughtered 1,800 of its people. In the north, the civil war was complicated during the war's last winter by Marshal Alexander's November 13, 1944, radio broadcast to the partisans north of the German Gothic line. The Allied commander instructed them to "cease large-scale activity" until the Anglo-Americans resumed their offensive in the coming spring. One can interpret Alexander's proclamation either as a tragic blunder or as a devious attempt to curtail partisan strength before the final Allied victory. In any case, it allowed the enemy to direct more of their energies in crushing the resistance and intensifying their reign of terror.

The Allied spring 1945 offensive sealed the Nazi and Fascist fate in northern Italy. Before the cannons opened up, however, the Germans had already inaugurated surrender negotiations with the Allies. Behind Mussolini's back, early in March General Wolff undertook serious secret talks in Switzerland, first with Allen Dulles, the head of the American Office of Strategic Services (OSS), and then with representatives of the Caserta headquarters. At about the same time, Germany's Gothic Line started to crumble before the Allied advance. Along a front that stretched from north of Rimini on the Adriatic across the peninsula to the mouth of the Arno River near Pisa, the collapse of the Reich in Italy began.

The Allies launched their final push on April 1, and the resistance quickly joined in the initiative. Ten days later the leaders of the Communist underground ordered preparations for the insurrection. Bologna was the first large city to fall on April 21, although when the Allies entered along its famous arcaded streets, they discovered that the Germans had already fled and left the city in partisan hands. Over the next week and a half, similar scenes were repeated in Genoa, Turin, and Milan. The formal German surrender did not occur until May 2.

On April 27, partisans caught Mussolini disguised as a German soldier and trying to escape. His wife, Rachele, had already found safety over the Swiss frontier; now the Duce led an entourage of blackshirt refugees that linked up with a retreating German convoy. Partisans halted the motorcade as it made its way north along the Lake Como shore road. News of the capture reached Milan where the resistance headquarters dispatched a special execution squad to deal with the Duce. The next day Mussolini was shot along with a small group of Fascists that included Party Secretary Pavolini and Achille Starace. Another victim was the Duce's mistress Claretta Petacci, who had caught up with him to share his fate. The corpses were carted to Milan's Piazza San Loreto, a place where Fascist Black Brigades had earlier heaped the remains of executed hostages. There, on the early morning of April 29, the Duce's cold body, Petacci's, and those of the others were dumped, beaten, and subjected to ghastly indignities. They were then hoisted upside down on ropes at a gas station, dangling like carcasses in a butcher shop.

Reprisals against Fascists became a serious problem across northern Italy, and perhaps eleven or twelve thousand of them perished by the so-called justice of the piazza through the summer of 1945. The zone around Modena in Emilia gained a particularly dubious fame as the "Triangle of Death" where not only Fascists but conservatives of any stripe feared for their lives before violence and retribution motivated by leftist revolutionary impulse. The Allies helped to defuse the situation by first honoring the partisans with liberation parades before ordering them to surrender their weapons. Far from everybody complied, and many guns remained hidden under beds or in cellars. Still, the number of extralegal retributions steadily diminished as 1945 drew to a close, and the strange calm of a numbed and defeated nation descended on Italy.

Notes

1. John Diggins, *Mussolini and Fascism: The View from America* (Princeton, N.J.: Princeton University Press, 1972), 335.

2. Angelo Del Boca, *The Ethiopian War, 1935–1941,* trans. P. D. Cummins (Chicago: University of Chicago Press, 1969), 59–60.

3. Denis Mack Smith, *Mussolini: A Biography* (New York: Random House, 1983), 222.

4. James MacGregor Knox, *Mussolini Unleashed, 1939–1941: Politics and Strategy in Fascist Italy's Last War* (Cambridge: Cambridge University Press, 1986,) 55–56).

5. Galeazzo Ciano, *The Ciano Diaries, 1939–1943,* ed. Hugh Gibson, (New York: Fertig, 1973), 264.

6. Roberto Chiarini, "Le origini dell'Italia repubblicana (1943–1948)," in *Storia d'Italia: 5. La repubblica, 1943–1963,* ed. Giovanni Sabbatucci and Vittorio Vidotto (Rome: Laterza, 1997), 16, 26.

Chapter 4
Christian Democracy and Prosperity

THE FASCIST APOCALYPSE AND THE HORROR OF WORLD WAR fought within its borders shook Italy as perhaps nothing else ever has in its modern history. Political chaos and international disgrace compounded death and physical destruction of titanic proportions. Within the ashes, however, some embers of hope glimmered. Italy would revive, but how much of the old nation would remain? What shape would the phoenix take?

Italy's traditional place at the low end of the industrial powers was made worse by the war's destruction and dislocation. By the end of the reconstruction in the mid-1960s, however, Italy had found its path toward becoming a modern society on par with France or Britain. Catholics, furthermore, rallied around a powerful new party, the Christian Democracy (*Democrazia Cristiana*, or DC), which would dominate politics for over four postwar decades. It would fight to resurrect and preserve some of the nation's ancient ways while somewhat paradoxically making the transition to a modern consumer culture and a flawed but sensible democracy.

Reconstruction provided the Catholics their opportunity to remake Italy. Unlike Liberalism and Fascism (and Marxism), which were preponderantly northern phenomena, the DC was anchored in the cultures of the two Italies, the industrial and European north and the agricultural and Mediterranean south. Before World War I, northerners had identified with Liberalism and Marxism more often than did southerners. Afterward, modernity in the 1920s was identified as a Fascist phenomenon that rooted itself in the north more successfully than it did in the Mezzogiorno, where many considered it an almost foreign imposition.

With the fall of Mussolini, the north became a cauldron of democratic and social ideas identified with the CLN coalition, especially its north Italian wing, the CLNAI. Italians dubbed this phenomenon the "Wind from the North," a blast of reform that blew down the peninsula just as Fascism had done twenty years before. The Wind reached Rome in June 1945 and took the shape of a CLNAI delegation that insisted on a new government for Italy to reflect its democratic and progressive aspirations.

Indeed, the south was suspicious of Parri and his new government, and most of the region aligned with traditional elements associated with the monarchy and the church. Consequently, after the end of the war, north and south had to compromise to put a new face on the nation. This visage was drawn mostly by the DC, a party that drew its strength from both the north and the south and would assume the role of mediator.

From CLN to Republic

In Rome, the CLN prime minister Ivanoe Bonomi stepped aside to accommodate the Wind by opening the way for the new government, formed on June 21, 1945, under the resistance leader, Ferruccio Parri. A Piedmontese economist who had opposed Fascism from the start, Parri endeared himself to resistance comrades under his nom de guerre, Zio Maurizio (Uncle Maurice), and he earned their respect by enduring both Mussolini's and Hitler's prisons before the liberation of Milan. There, he served as the reformist Action Party's representative to the Committee of National Liberation and, with Luigi Longo, one of Raffaele Cadorna's "vice commanders." In Rome, Parri's new ministry included figures from all CLN parties and all parts of Italy, but fourteen of its twenty members would be northerners.

Prime Minister Parri faced the daunting task of rebuilding his devastated nation. Mortality figures were not as terrible as those of World War I, but, at between four hundred thousand and five hundred thousand, they were bad enough. Still, war had been much harder on civilians in 1945 than it had in 1918. In other human tolls, moreover, 1945 was far worse. The refugee problem was enormous. One and one half million Italians had gone to work in Germany before the armistice, and another half million were sent there after 1943. The Allies, furthermore, still held over one million prisoners of war in camps from Kenya to Missouri, and stragglers from Italy's invasion of the Soviet Union would wander back home for years after the war's end. Homelessness was another pressing challenge. The minister for the reconstruction, Meiuccio Ruini estimated that, of Italy's thirty-one million dwellings, over six and one half million had been damaged or destroyed.

The national economy, furthermore, stood in shambles, with 1945's industrial output less than one-third of 1938's. In some sectors it even receded to nineteenth-century levels. Electricity was rationed. Transportation was a catastrophe with over half of Italy's locomotives destroyed, 46 percent of its freight cars and 17 percent of its passenger cars. The merchant marine in 1945 was one-tenth of its 1940 size. Such devastation had heartbreaking effects throughout a population that strained to survive. The journalist Curzio Malaparte, who had flirted with Fascism but also languished in Mussolini's jails, lamented of "Our misery, our physical and moral humiliation, and our despair."

Such formidable challenges overwhelmed Parri and tainted his administration with what the historian Paul Ginsborg has described as "the constant impression of being unable to cope."[1] Parri's calls for reforms were vague and moderate, but many misjudged him as a radical, guilty by association with the more fiery elements of the new coalition. The colleague who raised most eyebrows was Pietro Nenni, the Socialist who agitated for something approaching a social revolution. Parri placed Nenni in charge of the moribund High Commission for Sanctions against Fascism where he tried to sharpen the agency's weapons and, in October 1945, attempted to push the purge into the private sector. Consequently, by November the Parri government encountered an attack barrage from alarmed Center–Right factions within the CLN coalition led by the Liberals and from outside the cabinet by the *Uomo Qualunque* (UQ) movement, a force that captured postwar discontent over the CLN's sometimes preachy reformism.

The UQ was led by the unlikely figure of a dapper and monocled film critic, Guglielmo Giannini. Embittered by the loss of a son in the war, he appealed to the "man on the street" (the *uomo qualunque*), who saw little difference between Fascist and CLN rhetoric and branded them both as long-winded social engineers and hypocrites. Giannini directed fire on all of the CLN parties, and political cartoons in his newspaper portrayed the DC leader De Gasperi as a vulturelike creature in priestly garb, while Communists and Socialists, particularly the detested Nenni, were depicted in blackshirt.

The UQ and other anti-Parri factions inside and outside the CLN coalition enjoyed support from many in Anglo-American ranks who still wielded enormous power as occupation forces in northern Italy. The Italo-American banker Amedeo Giannini for example, visiting from San Francisco warned the Parri government in November to end the resistance threats against industry or suffer the consequences. Faced with attacks from so many quarters, the CLN cabinet crumbled. On the evening of November 24, a disheveled and angry Parri submitted his resignation to Crown Prince Umberto.

The collapse of the Parri government signaled the ascent of the Christian Democratic Party to the helm of the ruling CLN coalition. Alcide De Gasperi replaced Parri as prime minister on December 10, 1945. Like October 28–29, 1922 it was a turning point in Italian history. De Gasperi and the Catholics emerged from the political ghetto that they had occupied since the Italian army breached Rome's walls in 1870 and had rendered Pius IX the "prisoner of the Vatican." An ebullience rushed through Catholic ranks, where the failures of Liberalism and Fascism could be considered victories against secularism. In 1946, Archbishop Idelfonso Schuster of Milan, Italy's largest Catholic diocese, charged that "the idea of a secular state for us is a historical error and a national crime." Now, many felt, Italy could reclaim its Catholic roots.

Consolidated between 1945 and 1948, DC rule provided not only a philosophical challenge but also a stability that no other large Western democracy could claim during the postwar era. As Italy's first sincerely Catholic prime minister, De Gasperi was the initial link of an unbroken chain of DC premiers that would extend over thirty-five years until the Republican Giovanni Spadolini took the office in 1981. Even then the Christian Democracy maintained control over the legislature until the early 1990s. DC cabinets routinely formed and reformed so that single governments rarely lasted for more than a year and a half. But the Christian Democratic Party bosses maintained a musical chairs game that appeared less riotously chaotic than it did calmly or boringly repetitive. Most of the time only a handful served as prime ministers. De Gasperi held the office five times, as did Aldo Moro and Mariano Rumor. Amintore Fanfani headed six governments, and Giulio Andreotti chaired seven.

Opponents criticized the Christian Democracy as simply an anti-Communist organization or a party whose mission was merely to capture and keep power. While both analyses contained some truth, such characterizations were flawed in their denial of the DC's authentic ideology as a Catholic party. It was a new party whose roots paradoxically extended far deeper into the soil of Italy's history than did those of any other. Liberals and Marxists claimed Enlightenment traditions as theirs and the Fascists frequently portrayed themselves as the modern rejection of those ideas. But the Bible and ancient teachings of Christian Rome inspired the DC. As such, it never fit comfortably into East–West

Cold War debates, constrained by eighteenth- and nineteenth-century frameworks with which Marxists and Liberals were most accustomed. The DC's popularity, for instance, drew from the whole social spectrum in a way that most modern European parties did not, attempting to be almost all things to almost all people, all ranks and all corners of the nation. And it came close to doing so, attracting both white-collar, blue-collar, and peasant support and more women's votes than any other party. The DC even equaled Communist totals among working-class ballots. And it was a national party, with reliance on southerners, Roman bureaucrats, and much of the northern bourgeoisie. Lombardy, the Veneto, and the Trentino were key DC strongholds, and northern cities such as Bergamo and Vicenza, in fact, often delivered the highest percentages of DC votes.

But De Gasperi's ascent at the end of 1945 did not kill the CLN coalition. His first three cabinets, lasting through the spring of 1947, maintained the arrangement with representatives from most of the resistance factions. The Ministry of Grace and Justice, for example, was held by the PCI chief Palmiro Togliatti during the first cabinet and then by another Communist, Fausto Gullo, in the second and third. The minister of finance in De Gasperi's first two cabinets was the tough Communist and former purge chief, Mauro Scoccimarro. Pietro Nenni served in the first two, while his fellow Socialist, the more moderate Giuseppe Romita, was included in all three.

The DC and the Left parties, moreover, continued to agree on a number of issues. One matter that united them concerned the retention or rejection of the Savoy monarchy, a question decided in a June 1946 referendum. DC leadership, in fact, repudiated much of its own rank and file to join the Left in a successful campaign against the crown. Of the CLN parties only the Liberals worked to retain the monarchy. Outside the coalition, the UQ and makeshift royalist organizations fought for the king. The Vatican also lobbied on behalf of the Savoy. The Anglo-Americans, on the other hand, kept out of the controversy to the disappointment of many conservatives. But the United States had never supported the crown, while the British abandoned their commitment to it by June 1945 when Churchill stated that Italy's choice of democracy, once made, would render irrelevant the question of monarchy versus republic.

The CLN's resolve to rid Italy of the Savoys pushed the king at long last to do something. To present a fresh and less vexing option for the voters, Victor Emmanuel finally ended his reign of almost forty-six years and abdicated on May 9, one month before the referendum. Without even a word of thanks to his servants, the aged monarch and Queen Elena quietly sailed away to exile in Egypt. He died there shortly after, in 1947. Victor Emmanuel was succeeded by his son, Umberto II, the last king of Italy.

But abdication was a case of too little too late. Dubbed the "May King," Umberto fought to save his throne through an electoral campaign that appeared unseemly to some. Umberto's past, however, and his inescapable identification with his father worked against the Crown. His silence during the *ventennio* did not inspire any anti-Fascist support, and his lackluster role as lieutenant general of the realm upon the liberation of Rome did not change that. After the war, the Socialist Sandro Pertini promised Umberto with a lynching if he showed up in Milan; when the crown prince made the trip anyway, partisans strafed his villa with bullets. Queen Maria José had earned better credentials than her husband by her stronger personality and by her intrigues against Mussolini. But unfortunately for the House of Savoy, the referendum judged Umberto and his father, not her.

On June 2, 1946, Italian men and, for the first time, women, went to the polls and abolished the crown by a vote of 12.7 million to 10.7 million. Analysts took note of the one and a half million canceled ballots. Most surprising, however, was that the Savoy monarchy was still so popular and that the vote went along a clean north–south split. Every region south of and including Lazio (Rome) opted to retain the Royal House; while every northern region called for its expulsion. A few days later the defeated Umberto left for exile in Portugal. He died in 1983, and his body rests in the French Savoy, at the abbey of Hautecombe, along with twenty-seven of his ancestors. The Republic of Italy was proclaimed on June 18 and shortly afterward the Constituent Assembly elected the Neapolitan liberal Enrico De Nicola as the nation's acting president.

Along with abolishing the monarchy, the 1946 vote sent delegates to Italy's Constituent Assembly, the last direct legacy of the CLN. The DC captured the most seats, 207 of 556, while the Communists won 104, and the Socialists took 115. But fervent ideological rancor did not mar debates in the new assembly. All parties could and did agree on the constitution's preamble that Italy was to be a republic founded on work with a duty to assist the poor and the workers. Togliatti and the Communists, moreover, supported the DC's incorporation of the Lateran Pacts into the charter as its article 7. And all concurred that Italy's president would occupy a largely ceremonial position. *Ducismo,* the cult of the Duce, and the Fascist experience had soured everyone on the idea of strong executives; and the Constituent Assembly instead entrusted power in a president of the Council of Ministers, or prime minister, and bound the position closely to the parliament. Election to the Chamber of Deputies was determined by a system of proportional representation. The completed Italian constitution took effect on January 1, 1948.

The CLN harmony that facilitated the drafting of the constitution, however, was neither ubiquitous nor lasting. The rosy complexion of De Gasperi's first three CLN cabinets from December 1945 until May 1947 worried both Washington and conservatives in Italy. The prime minister and much of the DC leadership calmed those fears by expelling the Marxist Left from the cabinet on May 31, 1947. Historians and other observers of the Italian scene have searched for a smoking gun or a key moment to explain or lay blame for De Gasperi's catharsis. Many have pointed to his January 1947 trip to America where he received promises for U.S. aid. No real proof, however, has linked De Gasperi's actions to American enticements. Nevertheless, five months later the Christian Democratic prime minister reorganized his cabinet without Communists and Socialists. Earlier that May the French also expelled the Communists from their cabinet, but not the Socialists. Italian Communist Party members never again occupied ministerial positions although the Socialists remained out of governing coalitions only until 1962. As it turned out, the Catholics sent the Socialists into a temporary purgatory while they banished their Communist comrades to a permanent hell.

The left-wing parties of the old CLN coalition resented the Center–Right's successful gambit to freeze them out of the cabinet. Many among them even felt that the Roman government had sided more against them than against their old common enemies, the blackshirts. The purge of Fascists had fizzled by 1946, and the Republic was launched with an amnesty of most imprisoned blackshirts. That Togliatti composed the amnesty did not erase the fact that, by the end of the year, prisons housed more ex-partisans than ex-Fascists. Furthermore, in 1947 the DC's new interior minister, Mario Scelba, purged the police of partisan elements that had joined at the end of the war.

With their hopes for Italy slipping away, the frustrated Left could do little except take to the streets and voice their anger. Perhaps the most memorable confrontation occurred when Rome moved to replace Milan's prefect, Ettore Troilo. During the liberation, many prefectural offices vacated by the Fascists had been filled by CLNAI. figures who represented the toughest and most battle-scarred factions of the resistance. After the war, Rome acted to replace these "political" leaders with "career" bureaucrats, a process that worked to defuse the revolutionary impulse. At the end of 1947, the last to go was Milan's Troilo. Troilo had distinguished himself during the war as head of the Maiella Brigade, one of the most valiant units of the anti-Fascist struggle. He was an enormously popular figure on the Left and his removal brought widespread objections. On November 28, the PCI representative in Lombardy, Gian Carlo Pajetta, protested the decision by directing angry workers and ex-partisans in a general strike and an occupation of Milan's prefecture. But their actions worked no effect on the outcome. From Rome, Prime Minister De Gasperi and Togliatti coordinated efforts to urge moderation and the situation calmed.

The Troilo incident was one of the last moments of cooperation between Communists and Catholics. Soon afterward Moscow instructed the Italian Communist Party to abandon its policy of conciliation and adopt one of obstruction. On the other side, an undercurrent of suspicion had always traversed the DC's opinion of Bolshevism that was inspired in great part by papal pronouncements such as Pius XI's *Divini redemptoris* in 1937 that pointedly argued against Moscow's goal of undermining Christian civilization. In 1944, Pius XII dismissed any notion of Italian Catholics embracing communism, and in the 1948 elections, he charged that a vote against God was a mortal sin.

The 1948 Elections

Now in direct confrontation, the DC and the Marxist parties squared off for the national elections of April 1948. The contest has often been portrayed by partisans as a manichaean clash of good and evil, of irreconcilable ideas, of slavery versus freedom. The DC claimed to carry the banner of Christian civilization with the blessings of Pope Pius XII. Catholicism's ubiquitous parish, monastic, and welfare networks and its far-reaching web of lay organizations mobilized behind the DC against the Left. Through, for example, the Coldiretti agricultural league, the DC maintained a grip on the countryside outside the "red belt" that was the core of Communist rural strength through Tuscany, Umbria, the Marche, and Emilia Romagna. The church's greatest lay organization, however, was Catholic Action. The tireless and relentless president of its men's division, Luigi Gedda, launched a special flank, the Civic Committees, to get out the vote.

The United States also joined the campaign. Washington urged Italo-Americans to contact their relatives back in the old country and advocate a free and non-Communist Italy. Popular Hollywood stars were pressed to record messages in hopes of victory. Marshaled by Jay Lovestone and David Dubinsky, American labor formed a phalanx with British help to pry their Italian comrades from the Left. The newly formed Central Intelligence Agency, furthermore, used the Italian elections as an early test of covert actions, channeling secret funds for the defeat of Italian Marxism. Above board the United States replaced its big stick with a carrot labeled with a dollar sign. During the war, Franklin Roosevelt had promised a "New Deal for Italy" and in June 1945 acting secretary of state Joseph Grew reiterated America's goal "to strengthen Italy economically and politically."

U.S. aid began to flow into Italy, directly at first and then through the United Nations Rehabilitation and Relief Administration (UNRRA). Already, in the initial postwar years Washington's assistance totaled $2.2 billion. In June 1947, Secretary of State George Marshall funneled much of the operation into his European Recovery Program (ERP), or Marshall Plan, that released even more funds for Italy and for other European countries. By the time the program ended in 1952, Italy received about 1.4 billion Marshall Plan dollars, or 11 percent of the total across Western Europe. Eighty percent of the aid came as goods while the rest largely took the form of loans with easy payment arrangements. The ERP also required Italy to establish a counterpart fund equal to the dollar amounts that it received. All deliveries reached Italy with great public relations fanfare and with enticements that much more would follow—if the April elections went the right way.

On the other side, frequent problems plagued the Left's electoral designs. The Socialists and the Communists found enough common ground to renew their wartime "Unity of Action Pact;" and for the elections the two parties forged a "Popular Democratic Front" in December 1947. But the alliance came at a crippling cost to the Socialists. Already in early 1947, their ranks suffered when disputes erupted between the pro-Soviet Lelio Basso and party leader Nenni on one side and the moderate Giuseppe Saragat on the other. In January, Saragat walked out of the party's congress and took a large group of sympathizers with him. His breakaway faction, about one-third of the Socialist parliamentary bloc, dubbed itself the Socialist Party of Italian Workers (Partito Socialista dei Lavoratori Italiani, or PSLI), which soon renamed itself the Italian Social Democratic Party (*Partito Social-Democratico Italiano*, or PSDI). The fissure placed the weakened Nenni in a position subordinate to his ally Togliatti who promptly secured control of the Marxist-led labor front and co-operative societies from the Socialists. At its first congress in May and June of 1947 the monolith of organized labor, the Italian General Confederation of Labor (*Confederazione Generale Italiana del Lavoro*, or CGIL) elected the charismatic Apulian Communist Giuseppe Di Vittorio as its president. The moderate Left also lost a crucial independent faction in October 1947 when the Action Party voted to dissolve. Always plagued by contention and hurt by its poor showing in the 1946 elections, some *azionisti* moved to the Socialists, while the more centrist faction led by Parri landed in the new Republican Party.

International developments also hampered the left-wing cause. Joseph Stalin's sinister shadow darkened all of Eastern Europe and terrified many Italians. The ugly brutality and the drabness of Moscow's atheist and Communist empire dismayed many who refused to believe that the PCI could walk its own path independent of Kremlin dictates. It was no secret, for instance, that Togliatti had worked in Moscow through the 1930s and had only returned to Italy in 1944. Suspicions of Soviet machinations grew in September 1947 when the USSR established the Cominform and the PCI dutifully joined it. Its purpose, to coordinate Communist movements and parties around the globe, was essentially that of the old Comintern, which had disbanded during the war to save embarrassment among the Moscow–Washington–London allies.

In February 1948, five months after the birth of the Cominform and two months before Italy's April elections, attention focused on Czechoslovakia, where the Communists established a Soviet puppet dictatorship under Klement Gottwald. Their murder of the distinguished liberal foreign minister, Jan Masaryck, and the famous judgment attributed to Gottwald that the takeover was like slicing butter with a hot knife convinced many Italians that such brutal measures were not for them. The DC later captured these fears in a political poster that portrayed a surly Czech youngster who had earned party honors by ratting on his parents for subversive activity. Good Catholic children loved and obeyed their parents and were incapable of such fiendishness.

In the end, the April 1948 elections yielded the DC its sought-after triumph. The Catholics captured 48.5 percent of the popular vote, which yielded a razor-thin majority in the Chamber of Deputies. The DC trounced the Left, while no other centrist or conservative party came close to it. The Left coalition mustered only 31 percent while the small "lay" parties divided most of the rest: Saragat's Social Democrats took 7.1 percent; the Republican Party, where many ex-*azionisti* found a home, earned 2.5 percent; and 3.8 percent went to the Liberals. The Monarchists took 2.8 percent, and the neo-Fascist Italian Social Movement (*Movimento Sociale Italiano*, or MSI) captured a further 2 percent. The nuisance of Giannini's Uomo Qualunque, furthermore, had collapsed.

On July 14, the picture darkened more for the Left when a young student of right-wing sympathies wounded Palmiro Togliatti in an assassination attempt. Humbled in electoral defeat and frustrated by the attack on their leader the leftists confronted the police in the streets of Italy and suffered there as well. Catholic workers added salt to the wounds in the summer and autumn of 1948 when they severed their allegiance to Di Vittorio's CGIL. The break-away Catholics went on to form their own union and were followed by the Liberal workers who walked out in 1949. The 1948 election and its aftermath guaranteed that the Communists and Socialists would wander the political wilderness for the predictable future.

Enrollment in the Western Cause

DC victory in 1948 secured Italy's commitment to the anti-Communist struggle and identification with the Washington-led Western camp. But attachment to the Western alliance was not always smooth. The peace treaty, signed on February 10, 1947, indicated that Washington and London were still unprepared to accept

Rome with open arms, an embarrassment for the Christian Democrats and the whole CLN coalition, which felt a certain sting of
betrayal from the Allies. That Rome broke with Berlin in 1943 and
declared war on Germany two years before the end of the fighting
seemed to mean next to nothing. Furthermore, the treaty completely ignored the contribution of blood made by the resistance
to the defeat of Nazism and Fascism. Instead, the West appeared
to deal with Italy as if it were just any other defeated enemy.

The peace treaty required Italy to severely limit its armed
forces. Much of the fleet went to the Soviets and what remained of
its air force was practically eliminated. The document emphasized
Rome's obligation to pay reparations and, except for a United Nations Trusteeship over Somalia, stripped Italy of all overseas territories. The trusteeship ended in 1960 when, in union with British
Somaliland, Somalia achieved independence. In Europe, Italy held
its northern frontier with Austria but surrendered Briga and
Tenda to France, two small Alpine tracts with important hydroelectric stations. As in 1918, Italy's big border problem in 1945
was in the northeast, where Marshal Tito and his Yugoslav partisan fighters occupied Trieste and the Istrian peninsula. At the
war's conclusion, Tito honored Marshal Alexander's order to pull
out and transfer the city to Allied occupation although Yugoslavia
retained control of most of the Istrian hinterland. The peace
treaty did not resolve the Trieste issue that kept Italy on the front
line of the Cold War for the next decade.

Pressures raised by the peace treaty alleviated somewhat as the
Cold War worsened and dictated that Italy be included in the Western camp. So, in the long run the Allies would not condemn Rome
to wander the world in ignominy. While they disappointed nationalists in not keeping Tito out of Istria, the Anglo-Americans
eventually supported Rome's claim to Trieste that would reunite
with Italy in 1954. Furthermore, Washington, London, and Paris
ultimately waived their reparation demands.

Alignment with the Eastern bloc was so utterly out of the question that identification with the American camp seemed Italy's
only real option, but the argument grew murkier when the ques-

tion arose of Italian participation in a military alliance. The small pro-American "lay" parties—the Republicans, the Liberals, and Sazragat's Social Democrats—welcomed the idea, but such a daunting step gave pause even to many Catholics, to say nothing of Marxists. Factions in the U.S. State Department and Congress, moreover, joined with some Europeans to oppose Italian membership in an Atlantic alliance. After all, Italy, a member of the defeated Axis, was not even an Atlantic nation. A bit of roundabout sympathy came from Paris, but only for political reasons: to balance its own wish that the alliance include Algeria. The Western allies, however, could not reach an agreement on Italy, and none invited Rome to join. De Gasperi therefore submitted his own petition on March 1, 1949.

In the end, the Truman administration joined forces with pro-American Italians, particularly the republican foreign minister Carlo Sforza and the ambassador to Washington, Alberto Tarchiani, to win the day. Italy became a charter member of the North Atlantic Treaty Organization (NATO) on April 4, 1949. In June 1951, Naples became the headquarters for NATO's southern European forces responsible for the Mediterranean and Black Seas. NATO's land-based defense of Italy, itself, was placed under an Italian four-star general at Verona. And a southern European air command was established at Naples with subordinate commands at Vicenza and in Turkey.

Beyond political and military commitments, Italy was economically wedded to the capitalist west. Washington's substantial aid worked to draw Rome into its fold while the process of European integration started in 1951 when Italy joined France, West Germany, and the Benelux nations in the European Coal and Steel Community (ECSC). Prime Minister De Gasperi's "pro-European Policy" (the *politica europeista*) and his rapport with fellow Christian Democrats such as Chancellor Konrad Adenauer of West Germany facilitated this initial step toward a larger customs union. In 1955 at Messina, Italy hosted the other five members of the ECSC in preparation for the "Common Market" that saw the light of day via the Treaty of Rome in March 1957. At the end of 1955, furthermore, Italy entered the United Nations.

Just as crucial was De Gasperi's appointment in May 1947 of the Liberal Luigi Einaudi as both minister of finance and the budget. From 1948, when he succeeded Enrico De Nicola, until his death in 1955, he would be Italy's president. During the Fascist regime, the respected Piedmontese scholar taught at the University of Turin, and he founded Italy's *Review of Economic History* in 1935. After the war, he became the governor of the Bank of Italy. In his study of the reconstruction, John Lamberton Harper wrote that the enormous powers that Einaudi received provided for him "the opportunity to recast the domestic economy along liberal lines and link it to the world according to the precepts of comparative advantage."[2]

Einaudi took aim at Italy's rampant inflation fueled by easy credit and tightened the economy by the autumn of 1947 in a monetarist squeeze. Interest rates climbed as did the amounts of reserves that banks were required to hold. Einaudi's plans, calling for high unemployment rates and low wages, were maintained after he left his ministerial posts for the presidency. His policies recalled old nineteenth-century heartless liberalism by placing the burden of suffering on the working class and peasants, many of whom retaliated in the streets with tragic consequences. In the late spring of 1949, six peasants were killed in confrontations with Scelba's police; in October three died near Catanzaro; the next month, two more near Foggia; and in January 1950, six workers were shot to death and fifty more were wounded in Modena. Despite those tragedies, Einaudi's measures survived and led to greater confidence in the lira that stabilized at a rate of around 625 to the dollar, an exchange that would keep until the mid-1970s.

Labor trouble dogged the economy into the early 1950s, but by 1952, Italy's industrial production climbed to 140 percent over 1938's level, export figures rose, savings increased, and so did investments. The end of wartime restrictions were uneven but came in time. Train travelers, for example, enjoyed somewhat normal schedules by the autumn of 1945, but bread and pasta were not removed from the ration list until August 1950.

Fundamental disagreements persisted, however, between Catholic and capitalist visions of society and economy. Italian capitalists and their American allies were never entirely comfortable in their alliance with the DC. The party refused to be a factotum, or mouthpiece, for corporate bosses who generally felt more at home among Liberals or Republicans. And although important Christian Democrats such as Amintore Fanfani stressed compatibility between Catholicism and capitalism, Rome's suspicions of America's ideology, and its way of life remained a cultural problem. Papal criticisms of economic liberalism from Pius IX's reactionary "Syllabus of Errors" to Leo XIII's more moderate *Rerum novarum* to Pius XI's *Quadrigesimo anno* were taken seriously by serious Christian Democrats, and the DC, motivated by De Gasperi's dictum that it was a centrist party that leaned toward the Left, usually stood four-square behind unliberal visions of planned economy and the welfare state.

The DC also appealed to social conservatives and fought to maintain what it considered to be Italy's traditional and Catholic way of life. It opposed divorce and abortion and stood for a traditional vision of family and society. The DC identified leather-strap heartlessness with nineteenth-century liberalism and preferred its Christian mandate, inspired, at least in some good measure, by ideals of brotherly love and charity for the aid of distressed families and mothers.

The Christian Democracy conceded much to Liberal principles embodied in the Americans and Einaudi, but De Gasperi and much of the party leadership were anxious to apply some of their own Catholic and reformist economic principles to Italy. When he moved up to the presidential residence, the Quirinal Palace, Einaudi was replaced at the Treasury, Budget and Finance Ministries by the Catholics Giuseppe Pella and Ezio Vanoni. Prime Minister De Gasperi, moreover, eventually orchestrated the DC in promoting its own policies. Still, it took pressure from peasant land seizures and embarrassment by excessive police response to push Rome into action and many of the measures that turned Italy into a welfare state had to wait until the 1960s and 1970s.

Christian Democracy, moreover, intensified its day-to-day direction of the economy through political appointments in state-controlled businesses, particularly the IRI, the sprawling holdover from Fascism. In 1948, its planning staff, headed by Pasquale Saraceno, launched a bold five-year plan that called for extensive aid to the south. On July 11, 1950, Rome launched the Fund for the South (*Cassa per il Mezzogiorno*) to deal with southern poverty through the transfusion of billions of lire into its economy. The Cassa later extended its work to depressed zones in the north. The Sila Law of May 12, 1950, furthermore, expropriated underused land in Calabria and distributed it to poor peasants, measures extended across Italy in the *stralcio* legislation of September 21. In 1954, Budget Minister Vanoni announced that Italy's economy would aim at full employment, elimination of the gap between north and south, and eradication of the nation's balance of payments deficit.

Another state giant formed in 1953, the National Hydrocarbon Agency (*Ente Nazionale Idrocarbur*, or ENI) under the DC resistance hero and financial wizard Enrico Mattei. With De Gasperi's help, Mattei lobbied for the ENI to ensure that natural gas deposits discovered in the Po valley did not fall into the hands of private entrepreneurs but rather would be safeguarded in government hands for the commonweal. It was no small coincidence, however, that ENI production would be managed by the Christian Democracy. Created primarily for fuel industry ventures, the ENI soon diversified and even operated a newspaper, *Il giorno*. Mattei's ENI and the IRI were both entrusted to the new Ministry of State Holdings, created in December 1956 under Giuseppe Togni. The ENI became one of Italy's most dynamic public ventures, and Mattei's influence in the party grew until his premature and suspicious death in a plane crash in 1962.

Although Italy had turned the corner on its postwar road to recovery, as the 1950s began, it was still one of Europe's most traditional societies. In 1951, more laborers still toiled in agriculture than in any other economic sector: 42.2 percent worked the soil, as opposed to 32 percent in industry and 25.8 percent in the service sector. Poverty figures must have shocked many among Italy's comfortable *borghesia*. At the start of the decade, only 7.4 percent of homes operated with all three amenities of electricity, drinking water, and indoor lavatories. Disproportionate figures between north and south aggravated the situation: 5.8 percent of northerners lived below the poverty line, while between 45 and 50 percent of southerners did. Among the most famous examples of want in the Mezzogiorno was a large section of Matera, a southern provincial capital in Basilicata. Much of the town lived in miserable hovels and cave dwellings, *i sassi*, before a shamed Rome intervened to clear the place and relocate the population.

The 1950s, however, launched the Italian economy on a course of relentless expansion that would continue into the next decade. From 1951 through 1957, Italy's gross domestic product grew 5.5 percent each year; and from 1958 until 1963, the rate climbed to 6.3 percent. Leading the way was industrial production that climbed on the average 8 percent a year from 1949 until 1963. After a brief slump, Italy's figures bounced back and surpassed 6 percent again in 1967. Among the major industrial nations, only Japan did consistently better. This economic "miracle" may have resembled the expansion at the beginning of the twentieth century, but it was more profound. Its novelty was such that the Italians adopted a foreign word to describe it, "*il boom*."

"Il Boom"

Observers have debated the roots of Italy's remarkable postwar prosperity. Was it the result of Einaudi's policies, American aid, or Catholic management? The answer may be some unfathomable mix of all three. But few doubt that it ushered a modernizing and consumerist transformation that rested on a stable lira, cheap labor, and expanding export markets, particularly for those kinds of high-quality and luxury goods that Italy had specialized in for centuries.

The first signs of the good times were felt among the middle class. One indication was the increase of lower-level white-collar jobs from 1,970,000 in 1951 to 2,650,000 in 1961. The middle class in general expanded from 26 percent of the population in 1951 to 38 in 1971.

But the boom unevenly favored the top end of society. Cheap labor still distinguished the economy on the lower side, filling the factories and tenements. Workers, mainly southerners but many from the Veneto, left their homelands for the higher wages found elsewhere. Switzerland and Germany lured many out of the country, but more abandoned their fields and villages for urban working-class quarters in Italy itself. The number of cities with populations over 100,000 grew from 26 in 1951 to 45 in 1971. The north received over 85,000 migrants in 1958 and almost 205,000 in 1963, an exodus that aggravated old social problems. Seventy-percent of Italy's communes, virtually all smaller rural municipalities, lost population between 1951 and 1961, while whole areas of the Mezzogiorno, particularly Molise and Basilicata, lost more than 10 percent of their sons and daughters who left for work and better lives in the north and elsewhere. Their new realities, however, failed to measure up to their dreams of prosperity and comfort.

Neighborhoods expanded both horizontally and vertically on the outskirts of Italy's great northern cities. By 1958, for instance, Milan's suburbs equaled the city in population. Working-class quarters there, as well as those in Turin, Rome, and other cities, were dubbed the "*borgate*," squalid ecological disasters of slipshod and often illegal construction. The transplanted workers, furthermore, confronted northern cultural, and perhaps racial, bigotry. One poll taken in Turin revealed this problem in which 61.8 percent of the newcomers to the city welcomed the chance to mix with natives as relatives or friends. On the other hand, 42.6 percent of established Torinesi rejected such arrangements with Campanians and 53.3 percent considered associations with Calabrians as distasteful.

At the same time, Italians somehow became healthier and lived longer than their parents. In 1940, men lived on average for fifty-nine years, while two decades later the figure reached sixty-eight. In the same period, women's life spans rose from sixty-three to seventy-three years. Improved hygiene accounted for a massive drop in deaths from infections and parasites: from 265 for every 100,000 people in 1921 to twenty per 100,000 in 1965. At the same time, more suffered from the kinds of diseases found in the satisfied nations. Deaths from circulatory problems climbed from 212 per 100,000 in 1921 to 316 per 100,000 in 1965.

Extended and healthier lives were facilitated or enhanced by a new wealth of consumer goods and labor-saving devices. Whereas 4 percent of Italian families owned washing machines and 14 percent possessed refrigerators in 1951, by 1965, those figures rose to 23 and 55 percent. Radio ownership crested in the late 1950s at about six million. During the same years, television started its take off. National service was inaugurated by the state-owned RAI system in 1954 and by 1958 Italians owned over one million sets, a figure that sextupled by 1965.

Prosperous Italy took to the road in the 1950s and 1960s. FIAT facilitated the drive to drive by introducing its inexpensive "600" model in 1955, and on May 19 of the following year, President Giovanni Gronchi laid the first stone of the nation's expressway system at San Donato Milanese. Car ownership exploded from 342,000 in 1950 to over four and a half million by 1964 and almost five and a half million in 1965, a nearly sixteenfold increase. Motor scooters experienced roughly the same rate of growth with the enormously successful Vespas and Lambrettas leading the way. Remarkably, the amount of train passengers did not suffer a mirror-image decline, dropping from 386 million in 1951 to 321 million in 1965. At the same time, traffic deaths only doubled, from 4,266 in 1952 to 8,990 in 1965. Perhaps growing congestion on Italy's streets made driving more frustrating but safer.

The good times attracted foreign tourists and expatriates, charmed by the character of ancient city centers that the Italians wisely took great care in preserving. Outside of exceptions like Gio Ponti's Pirelli building in Milan, skyscrapers rarely cast shadows over urban skylines. In Rome no tower could reach higher than the dome of St. Peter's Basilica. With a few tragedies, Genoa's waterfront for example, expressways did not ruin historic urban centers like they did in the United States. In the 1960s, Bologna led the way in historic conservation, the first to implement national measures enacted in 1963. Five years later the city inaugurated Italy's first pedestrian zone.

Tourism flourished. In 1938, 269,000 people came to Italy by boat. The 1965 total was 703,000, a figure overshadowed by air travel that fast overcame ship traffic. By 1965, over ten million travelers passed through the nation's airports. In 1960, Rome welcomed visitors to the Olympic Games with its new Leonardo Da Vinci Airport at suburban Fiumicino. Not to be outdone, four years later Milan unveiled the nation's best subway system. Increased tourist demands required more facilities to lodge visitors. In the ten years after 1955, the number of Italy's hotels and *pensioni* grew from 11,555 to 22,266 while the amount of rooms shot from 247,794 to 530,144. Glamorous jet-setters behind sunglasses flocked to Italy and sank roots from Mediterranean villas to Venetian barstools. America's first lady Jacqueline Kennedy's 1962 jaunt on the Amalfi coast, for instance, became a media event covered by the international press and by the notorious Italian *papparazzi* photographers who dogged the ever-growing throng of celebrities.

Much of Italy's attractiveness remained in the quality and abundance of its art treasures, a prestige cultivated after the Fascist experience and World War II. Along with the museums, churches, palaces, and ruins, a particularly intense new arena took shape in the development of neorealist film. An attempt to blend social criticism with a gritty style that sometimes employed amateurs without scripts, early steps toward neorealism had been taken under the Fascists in their experimental film workshops, and in the art of some pioneers like Alessandro Blasetti. But Luchino Visconti's 1942 *Ossessione* and, above all, Roberto Rossellini's *Roma, città aperta* (*Rome, Open City*) of 1945 established the form as a force. Applauded by most critics who also endorsed the genre's leftist message, the movement, however, ran out of steam by the end of the 1940s. Its Marxist sympathies were out of touch with much of the population, and, rarely known for laughter and song, neorealist cinema was too oppressively serious in a war-weary world.

The public made clear its preference for less experimental products from Hollywood or from the more commercial Italian studios. The most successful "political" fare on Italian screens was probably the popular "Don Camillo" series of films that starred the French comic Fernandel. Based on Giovanni Guareschi's delightful stories that pit a parish priest, "Don Camillo," against the town's Communist mayor, "Peppone," the tales put human and sympathetic faces on a subject that many otherwise avoided. Neorealist literature was another story. Distinguished by such figures as Alberto Moravia and Leonardo Sciascia, it continued as a vital and innovative force well into the 1960s.

Western styles and comportment linked with modernization and a general embourgeoisement to affect social change. Family size shrank, keeping more in line with other developed nations of Europe and America. The average Italian household contained 4 people in 1951 and 3.3 in 1971. In the same period, families with five or more members declined from 33.3 percent of the total to 21.5. The downward slope coincided with a new model of a more independent Italian woman: working in the office, zipping around on motor scooters, and heading for the seashore. Not only did young and unmarried women seem to be enjoying themselves more, the proliferation of home appliances benefited their typically more sedate older sisters.

Christian Democrats and the church reacted ambivalently to the changing roles of women but attempted to stem the secular tide with uneven success. The hard-headed interior minister Mario Scelba waged war on bikinis, but the slinky costumes appeared on beaches anyway in greater and greater numbers. Another famous challenge came in 1956 when Pietro Fiordelli, the bishop of Prato, berated a local couple who were joined in a civil marriage but without the blessings of the church. He ordered their parish priest to denounce them from the altar as "public sinners," denied them the sacraments, and scolded their mothers and fathers "as gravely remiss in their duty as Christian parents."[3] Fiordelli, himself, however, became the center of a media storm in which most of the lay and left-wing press tarnished him as a crank and a hopeless prude. Fiordelli's comments brought him a nominal court fine that was forgiven in appeal.

Although divorce was becoming an issue of public debate, the Catholics kept the government from taking action on it through the 1950s and into the 1960s. Their attempt to hold the line on censorship met with less success. A number of censorship laws were issued from 1949 until 1965 that may have slowed but did not halt the exhibition of either pornographic works or Hollywood fare that was condemned for glamorizing divorce and violence. Deals between the Motion Picture Export Association of America and its Italian counterpart, the National Association of Cinematographic and Audiovisual Industries (Associazione Nazionale Industrie Cinematografiche Audiovisive, or ANICA), however, succeeded in reducing the number of American films shown in Italy, from 668 in 1948 to 150 in 1962.

Crisis in the Christian Democracy

Christian Democrats found that as life got easier during the "boom" years, it got more difficult for the party whose grip on the reins of power started to slip. The decline of the Communist menace, the erosion of the party's peasant–farmer constituency and, consequently, their votes, all contributed to the malaise. Success, furthermore, contained some of the seeds of the DC's trouble. Sitting atop Italy's political heap for so long, it controlled, by one estimate, forty thousand government agencies, ministries, commissions, and offices. The more gigantic of these state concerns, like the IRI or the Cassa per il Mezzogiorno, channeled enormous amounts of money and became breeding grounds for corruption and the abuse of power. The embarrassment of riches, however, was not confined to Christian Democrats. Depending on the parliamentary coalition, they doled out lucrative fiefdoms to their partners. Further down the food chain, for example, the Social Democrats fed on large portions of provincial tourist boards. The system was in place, but it would take decades for the magnitude of the corruption to surface.

The DC's troubles began when electoral defeat in 1953 ended its parliamentary majority. The Catholics came to that vote with two great burdens. First, the death of Joseph Stalin in the Soviet Union lessened Cold War tensions. The terror instilled by his regime pushed many, particularly conservatives, to seek collective strength and shelter in the DC. But with Stalin out of the picture, the idea that the Moscow might be guided by reasonable people muted the alarm bell and allowed less anxious voters to desert Christian Democracy's big umbrella.

The DC's other burden in the 1953 election was more of its own doing. De Gasperi and Party Secretary Guido Gonnella introduced an electoral reform plan wherein any government coalition that captured over 50 percent of the vote could claim two-thirds of the seats in the Chamber of Deputies. The proposal looked too much like the Fascist Acerbo Law of 1923 and backfired as a colossal blunder. Rival parties dubbed it the "*legge truffa*," or "swindle law." The name stuck, and the DC total sank to 40.1 percent of the 1953 vote, still the largest tally by far among the parties, but requiring coalitions and compromises with smaller factions of the Center and Right, usually the Social Democrats, Republicans, or Liberals. De Gasperi retired from politics and died shortly thereafter.

The next election in 1958 maintained the DC as Italy's largest party with 42.3 percent of the vote compared to 22.7 for the PCI and the Socialists' 14.2. But its plurality forced it again to fish for partners, keeping the DC at the perpetual mercy of its political allies. Accordingly, many in the party's progressive wings, led by the new Party Secretary Fanfani and his successor, Aldo Moro, pressured for an *apertura alla sinistra*, an "opening to the Left," that would take the Socialists into government coalitions as junior partners.

For their part the Socialists, too, were ready for a rapproche-
ment with the Christian Democrats and the chance to get back
into the government. Estrangement with the Communists was
easy after Stalin's death, particularly after the USSR's new party
chairman Nikita Kruschev laid bare his predecessor's horrors in
his "Secret Speech" of February 1956. His revelations combined
the following October and November with Moscow's violent response to the Hungarian uprising and shook Left solidarity to its
core. Even Togliatti began to distance himself from Moscow and
spoke of polycentrism, while the Socialists took the opportunity
to break with Togliatti.

The *apertura* assumed a critical importance in Italian politics
and all sectors registered their opinions. Business was split. Support for the plan came from FIAT and the state-controlled industries, while the ranks of the manufacturers' association, Confind-
ustria, were suspicious of it. At the Holy See, the death of the
conservative Pius XII in 1958 and the election of the Lombard
Angelo Roncalli to the Throne of St. Peter signaled fresh attitudes
more open to experiments like an "opening to the Left." Reflecting
the new attitude Roncalli, as Pope John XXIII, launched the reformist Second Vatican Council and entrusted it to bring the
Catholic Church up-to-date with modern society. Another push
for an *apertura* came from Washington in 1960 when John F.
Kennedy's electoral victory as president of the United States signaled less American resistance to Socialist participation in Rome's
government.

The next move came on February 21, 1962, when Fanfani
formed a government with Social Democrats and Republicans
that relied on Socialist support. On December 4 of the following year, after a brief, exclusively DC, or "*monocolore*," government under Giovanni Leone, Moro took the big step and
formed a cabinet containing Socialist members. A consequence
of the *apertura* was the nationalization of the electricity industry, an act that alarmed many sectors. As arguments over the
"opening" continued, some on the Right panicked. The head of
the Carabinieri, General Giovanni De Lorenzo, spun a conspir-

atorial web for a coup, but it was a stillborn plot and discovered only in 1967.

The essential consequence of the "opening to the Left," however, was to maintain Christian Democratic rule. New Socialist allies were allowed a place at the table, and the public trough, but PSI policies were not far removed from what the DC wanted anyway. In fact, during the debate over nationalizing electricity, another fight erupted over even more radical urban planning measures that were proposed not by a Socialist but by Fiorentino Sullo, the DC minister of public works.

The *apertura*, however, left many disgruntled. Catholic social conservatives would long remember it as the moment when the DC lost its soul to the short-sighted lure of compromise and party politics. Others who hoped that the Center–Left would usher in a new era of governance would also be disappointed at the lack of real change.

Still, regardless of Rome, change in the Italy of the 1960s was accelerating. Industrialization created new wealth. Significant numbers of southern and Veneto peasants had moved into the chaotic and inadequate housing of northern cities while leaving a vacuum in their home towns and regions. Everything from increased road traffic to skyrocketing school and university enrollments strained the system. Magazines and journals of opinion debated the problems of libertine lifestyles and delinquent youth, those with too much money and leisure time on their hands or who succumbed to the temptations of the new commercial culture.

The filmmaker Federico Fellini criticized the "sweet life" in his controversial work of 1960, *La dolce vita*. Although many Catholics condemned what they considered to be the film's bad taste, they could not deny its fairly conservative message: that Italy was changing at a substantial cost to its soul. The old fights between Mario Scelba and bikini-clad young ladies, between Guareschi's Don Camillo and Peppone, seemed charming in retrospect; but perhaps they foretold the advent of a powerful new consumer culture that was bursting the seams of an outdated political system.

Notes

1. Paul Ginsborg, *A History of Contemporary Italy: Society and Politics 1943–1988* (London: Penguin, 1990), 89.

2. John Lamberton Harper, *America and the Reconstruction of Italy, 1945–1948* (Cambridge: Cambridge University Press, 1986), 135.

3. P. Vincent Bucci, *Chiesa e Stato: Church–State Relations in Italy within the Contemporary Constitutional Framework* (The Hague: Martinus Nijhoff, 1969), 37.

Chapter 5

Toward the Twenty-first Century

FROM THE MID-1960S TO THE LATE 1970s, a chain of crises jeopardized Christian Democratic hegemony and the stability of the Italian republic. Student and labor unrest was joined by the actions of angry radical elements on both the Left and the Right that emerged to harass and destabilize the state, a nightmare of terrorism known as the "years of the bullet" (or, literally, "years of lead").

In the 1980s, massive scandals and international developments then affected Italy's course. The DC and its coalition allies somehow held on and rode out the bumpy ride until the century's last decade when an avalanche of corruption revelations pushed the whole political system over the brink. The Communist Party tumbled first, independently of the scandals but rather as a consequence of collapse of the Berlin Wall and Soviet power. Then it was the Socialists' turn and that of the DC, itself, prompting many to refer to the end of a "first" and the start of a "second" Italian republic.

The global consumer revolution also contributed to re-making Italy at the dawn of the third millennium, a phenomenon that may prove to be of the greatest significance. A relatively peaceful development but one of momentous consequence, its cultural and social repercussions have been factors of decisions reached more than ever in boardrooms around the world, from Milan to Frankfurt to Los Angeles. No longer an agricultural nation, Italy's industrial workforce also crested around 1970, leaving a predominantly service-oriented economy that resembled those of the most advanced nations. An influx of new workers from the Third World also distinguished the new economy, workers who often took many of the least lucrative jobs that nobody else wanted. Prosperity, however, could be observed in homes across the country, Italians comfortably situated before television and computer screens with more soft drinks and potato chips in their diet and less pasta and wine—a full consolidation of bourgeois, consumer, and postmodern culture with all its blessings and ills.

Culture and the Italian way of life seemed in danger of blurring into the international consumer model, barely distinguishable from that found in any other industrialized nation. The children of those who, only fifty, sixty, and seventy years before, watched German, English, and American tourists sun themselves at Capri and Taormina now traveled to Florida and Bangkok with the same tan in mind. By 2002, the Italians lived in a consumer nation—wired and on the jet.

Upheavals of the Late 1960s and Beyond

The unrest that distinguished the last thirty or so years of the twentieth century surfaced first in Italy's schools and factories. The nation's educational structure had hardly changed since the 1920s when Giovanni Gentile reformed it along Fascist lines. After decades of neglect, it now groaned under old elitist notions that barred most students from the prestigious high schools (the *licei*) and universities. In 1951, 12.6 percent of Italian adults had never even been to school, and 46.3 percent had not finished primary school. Thanks to two prosperous decades and government measures such as a 1962 reform aimed at keeping students in classes through age fourteen, by 1971, those figures dropped to 5.2 percent and 27.1 percent.

Rome successfully filled more classroom seats, but it failed in the next step of taking care of the students and soon discovered that the system was overworked. *Liceo* enrollments had climbed from 159,543 in 1951 to 288,659 by 1965 but the number of teachers did not keep pace, inching from 17,141 to only 20,285. The universities witnessed an even greater strain when regular full-time (*in corso*) enrollments more than doubled, from 142,722 in 1951 to 297,783 in 1965 and then to almost one half million by 1969. Squeezes on libraries, on professors, and on students proved too much and resulted in protests, riots and, short-lived campus occupations.

The education crisis magnified discontent with Italy's mainstream parties. Those on the far Left first felt betrayed by the Socialists when they joined the DC coalition in the early 1960s. Communism seemed paralyzed in eternal opposition during Luigi Longo's leadership from Togliatti's death in 1964 until Enrico Berlinguer succeeded him in 1972. Angry radicals then criticized Berlinguer's willingness to strike deals with the DC in order to end the PCI's exile. The party picked up votes during these years, but instead of taking the opportunity to challenge the Christian Democrats, Berlinguer aimed to join them as partners in a "*compromesso storico*," or "historic compromise." Disheartened, many radicals opted to leave the PCI and form independent factions, often fringe groups that identified with the Third World liberation struggles of Che Guevera and Ho Chi Minh.

The Marxist Left was not the only wellspring of opposition to the Roman status quo. Leftist Catholic factions also coalesced, inspired by the reforms of the Second Vatican Council and the pontificates of John XXIII and Paul VI. The latter's 1967 encyclical, *Populorum progressio*, for example, urged social and economic justice on a global scale. It is significant that the wave of campus occupations started in November of that year at two institutions with strong Catholic traditions: the University of Trent, founded only five years earlier by the Christian Democrats, and Milan's Catholic University of the Sacred Heart. The movement crested in January 1968 when thirty-six universities were occupied; and in

February when violence erupted at the "Battle of the Valle Giulia" near the University of Rome's School of Architecture.

Working-class discontent dovetailed with the student protests to compound the state's headaches. The labor crisis served to emphasize that the *dolce vita* had skirted through society and left large sectors untouched. Poverty remained a serious issue. In Rome, for example, tens of thousands still lived in shacks, and between one-quarter and one-third of the capital's residents dwelled illegally, mostly in squalid and unauthorized housing found in the suburban "*borgate*" ring around the city.

The problem was aggravated by a more sporadic economy after 1963 and a wage disparity between the public and private sectors. Through the 1950s and early 1960s, Christian Democratic managers of the giant state concerns, trained with Catholic social teachings, paid much higher salaries to their workers than did their counterparts in private industry. The latter soon faced demands from labor and felt obliged to catch up to the Catholic standards raising wages under pressure although inflation climbed as well, cutting into savings.

The workplace calm that persisted through most of the late 1950s and 1960s shattered when labor undertook both organized and wildcat strikes that reached a climax in the "Hot Autumn" of 1969. Restless student groups joined the workers to push the discussion from better wages and working conditions to questions of revolution and radical structural change.

Protests, strikes, and lockouts spread across Italy—from the Pirelli works at Milan and shipyards in Genoa and Trieste, where trouble had brewed since 1967, to the Porto Marghera petroleum plant near Venice and steel works in Taranto. Events crescendoed in July 1969 at FIAT's gigantic Mirafiori works near Turin. There, beneath banners that proclaimed a desire to control "everything," the workers clashed with police and fanned a revolutionary moment that extended beyond the factory walls.

A number of major national contracts were signed in December that granted the bulk of labor's demands, and most of the workers settled for the concrete gains achieved. From 1969 to

1973, hourly industrial wages almost doubled, while other re-forms enhanced the status of organized labor. In 1972, further-more, Italy's largest union, the Marxist CGIL agreed to a loose federation with the Catholic Italian Confederation of Workers Unions (*Confederazione Italiana Sindacati Lavoratori*, or CISL) and the Republican–Social Democratic Italian Labor Union (*Unione Italiana del Lavoro*, or UIL), reviving an old pact that had collapsed under the strains of 1948. These gains, however, only checked revolutionaries who had more ambitious adventures in mind and resorted to terrorism.

Terrorism

Leftist terrorism may have been the most notorious form of the violence that plagued Italy into the early 1980s, but it hardly com-prised the whole picture. International tension, for example, ac-counted for part of it. Proximity to the Middle East, in particular, brought Italy into contact with violence, the deadliest examples of which occurred in December 1973 at Rome's Fiumicino Airport where a botched hijacking of a Pan-Am jet caused the death of thirty-one victims. In December of 1985, furthermore, Palestinian gunmen murdered fifteen and wounded seventy-four innocents at the international terminal in an attack that was coordinated with another massacre at the Vienna airport.

From the early 1980s into the 1990s, furthermore, the Mafia and other organized criminal elements responded to a govern-ment crackdown by launching a reign of terror in Sicily. Their vengeance spread to the mainland in the early 1990s with such outrages as bombings at Rome's Cathedral of St. John Lateran and Florence's Uffizi Museum.

On the political Right, frustrated neo-Fascists who had been locked out of power since the Second World War II also emerged with blood on their hands. Their chief political vehicle had been the Italian Social Movement (*Movimento Sociale Ital-iano*, or MSI), named thus because even the label "Fascist" had been declared illegal, a status that well reflected the MSI's pariah world. No postwar coalition permitted MSI participation, and no postwar cabinet contained an MSI member. Only once at the national level, in 1960, did a DC government overtly court the cooperation of the MSI. Prime Minister Fernando Tambroni arranged that during parliamentary votes of confidence, neo-Fascist deputies abstain from casting their ballots against his government. The public outcry was immediate and bloody, with major riots in Rome, Genoa, Emilia-Romagna, and Sicily. The government collapsed, and the Christian Democrat Tambroni died a broken man soon after. The MSI crept back into its political ghetto, condemned in impotence with a perpetual 4 or 5 percent of the vote, a fate that the radical fringe refused to accept.

One disgruntled neo-Fascist was Prince Valerio Borghese, the commander of an elite Salò naval unit during the war. In December 1970, Borghese attempted to topple the government in a coup d'état, but his plan was hopelessly ill prepared and amounted to a few hours occupation of the Interior Ministry. Other neo-Fascists undertook more lethal adventures. Estranged from the MSI, which they considered irreparably compromised, some radical factions broke to form their own underground. Their terrorism frequently consisted of deadly bombings: at Milan's Piazza Fontana in 1969, in the attack on the *Italicus* express train in 1974, and with the Bologna train station massacre in 1980 that claimed the lives of eighty-four victims.

On the Left, many who remained dissatisfied or alienated after the upheavals of the late 1960s coalesced into splinter clusters. Some, like *Lotta Continua* ("The Struggle Continues"), maintained themselves out in the open of the legally sanctioned public square, while others went underground. Among these, the most significant terrorist organization was a force called the Red Brigades (*Brigate Rosse*, or BR). From both Marxist and Catholic roots, the Brigades sprang in the late 1970 as "autonomous workers organizations . . . ready to fight the bosses and their lackeys on their own grounds as equals."[1] Their assault was intended to create a violent tension that would push Italy over the brink into revolution. By 1974, they acquired a jacobin fame, declaring war on the state and accelerating a program of kidnapping and shootings.

In 1977, after it almost seemed that police pressure had extinguished the movement, the Red Brigades resurfaced with a vengeance. The closer that the PCI and the DC came to their historic compromise, the more intense became BR violence. The Communists in turn joined the Catholics to voice their disdain for the Red Brigades, as did organized labor, which resented their goal of cracking rank-and-file loyalty. The Brigades intensified their campaign to destabilize Italian democracy by striking at its core, assassinating well-placed government and business leaders, judges, and journalists or by crippling their victims by shooting them in the knees. The Christian Democratic government reacted forcefully in a mobilization that gave Italy the look of a police regime, a state of siege welcomed by the Brigades.

BR terror reached its zenith when it claimed as its victim the five-time prime minister Aldo Moro. On the DC's moderate Left, Moro had played a central role in the "opening to the Left" with the Socialists. Now he was working on a similar arrangement with the Communists, the historic compromise. In late February 1978, Moro convinced his DC colleagues to take the first step and support a new government that would exist thanks to PCI abstention. On March 11, Giulio Andreotti formed a *monocolore* cabinet, one with only DC ministers but which relied on support from the Republican, Socialist, Social Democrat, and Communist Parties. The maneuver enraged sectors across the political spectrum, from the far Right and DC conservatives to the U.S. government and to the extremist Left.

Five days later, the BR responded by ambushing Moro. On the morning of March 16, after he attended Mass, the DC leader and his five bodyguards sped down from the comfortable Monte Mario neighborhood toward central Rome. At a quiet intersection their two vehicles became hemmed between cars driven by BR members. Others, some disguised as airline pilots waiting at a bus stop, descended on the stalled motorcade in a hail of bullets. The terrorists yanked Moro from his car and shoved him into one of theirs while they killed all of his bodyguards.

The abduction of Aldo Moro launched a fifty-four-day ordeal that shocked and deeply scarred Italy's political life. The BR kept Moro hidden in a secret "People's Prison" from which they periodically released photos of their captive along with letters that he purportedly wrote in desperation. Supported by the Socialist Party and some friends in the DC, Moro's family took to the airwaves, imploring the government to negotiate his release. With Communist support, however, Christian Democratic leadership reluctantly opted for unconditional and immediate liberation. On April 21, the ailing Pope Paul entered the furor and publicly begged the Red Brigades to free his old friend. On his knees, the pontiff prayed that "a victorious sentiment of humanity still resides in your souls." But not even Paul's prayers could save Aldo Moro.

The captive's last communiqués turned bitter until April 25 when he expressed his wish to exclude from his funeral any government or official Christian Democratic representatives. On May 9, Moro's corpse was discovered crumpled in the trunk of a car parked in Rome roughly equidistant from DC and PCI headquarters. A shocked nation watched as Moro's angry wife took him home for a private burial in the earth of his native Apulia. Italy exploded in a recriminatory anger and a frustration that Rome and all of its resources had been powerless against the terrorists.

The Moro kidnapping and the 1980 Bologna train station attack marked the height of terrorism in Italy and the beginning of its end. With support from the PCI and the United States, Rome launched a successful antiterrorist offensive that, by 1979, put 259 leftist terrorists and 1,812 right-wing terrorists in prison, either convicted or awaiting trial. By December 1981, when the American general James Dozier was kidnapped, the BR campaign took a final downward turn. Captured Brigade leaders began to inform on their comrades and the crime was foiled by a joint Italo-American action. Although more would suffer attacks in the next few years, the Red Brigades had become a broken force.

New Forces

Along with the disruptions of underground factions, new forces served to complicate and democratize Italy's political life. Groups ignored during the economic, cultural, and social transformation of the 1950s and 1960s now demanded to have their voices heard.

One new faction in the mid-1960s was the Radical Party (*Partito Radicale*, or PR) of Marco Pannella. The PR and later the "Pannella List" distinguished the next three decades of Italian politics with outlandish measures taken to discredit the status quo. The Radicals upset Parliament, for instance, by electing Toni Negri who had been implicated with the Red Brigades, or Ilona Staller, better known by her pornographic film name, Cicciolina. By engaging his politics as theater, Pannella called into question fundamental assumptions of Italian democracy.

Pannella and the Radicals may have been most effective in their crucial alliance with nascent feminist groups—important although complex forces. Like the "boom," the women's movement did not affect all women in the same way. It frequently left behind poor rural women, for example. The American Anne Cornelisen observed the absence of any kind of liberation when she moved into a depressed southern village in the late 1950s to chronicle the bleak and desperate existence of its women. "There is no gay camaraderie in this poverty," she wrote almost twenty years later, "These people are born knowing they have no expectations."[2]

Urban women enjoyed more opportunities and labor-saving material benefits from the postwar prosperity although they, too, lagged behind their counterparts in northern Europe and in the United States. This lag was also true of organized feminist movements. Some small groups surfaced before World War I, and a few went beyond the middle-class reformism of Countess

Gabriella Spalletti Rasponi's National Council of Italian Women.

Before and perhaps even during the Fascist regime, the Catholic Church was the most successful force to mobilize women, although its accomplishments were ambiguous. Catholic women tended to be less feminist in the traditional or ideological sense of the word, although they were crucial to the church's political action. Princess Cristina Giustiniani Bandini established a women's wing of Catholic Action in 1908 and a girls' group formed in 1918 under Armida Barelli. Signals, however, continued to be mixed. Pope Pius XII's elocution of October 1945, for instance, urged women to become more involved in public issues while Prime Minister De Gasperi still spoke condescendingly of leading women to democracy.

By the end of the 1950s, other groups such as the women's division of the Catholic Labor Unions and the independent Catholic *Centro Italiano Femminile* adopted feminist stands on par with most secular groups. On the other hand, Italy's largest circulation magazine was the traditionalist *Famiglia Cristiana*, which, for the most part, emphasized women as mothers and wives and advocated such causes as pressuring the state radio, RAI, to perform the rosary over the air and, or advocating the canonization of Maria Goretti, a young girl who had been martyred in a brutal rape and murder.

The Left was initially slower to organize women. A feminist current ran through the prewar anti-Fascist resistance, and Marxist exiles in Paris published *Noi donne* ("We Women") between 1937 and 1939. The review relocated to Italy after the liberation of Naples, where it resumed printing in 1944. That same year the Communists organized a Union of Italian Women (*Unione di Donne Italiane*, or UDI), although Togliatti's speech to their inaugural meeting revealed only a tentative acceptance of equality between the sexes, cautioning his female comrades not to lose their femininity. The Union of Italian Women and *Noi donne* continued to serve as the voice of orthodox Marxism in the feminist movement.

The student and labor protests, followed by the divorce and abortion battles, stimulated a new kind of feminism along Western and secular models in the 1960s and 1970s. Among the first new groups, the small DEMAU formed in December 1965 in Milan to advocate the "de-mystification of male authority." Others followed. In 1970, the *Rivolta Femminile* (Female Revolt) was born, and one year later Rome hosted the first congress of the *Movimento di Liberazione delle Donne* (Women's Liberation Movement), an offspring of the Radical Party that would play a central role in the debates of the next decade. Other groups and journals followed to pressure for reform. The review *DWF*, for example, emerged as one of the chief forums for feminist discourse in the 1980s and 1990s. The historian Paul Ginsborg concluded that by 1975, the women's movement had assumed national proportions, and feminist dimensions started to integrate themselves into all questions in the public arena.[3]

By the early 1980s, something of a calm returned to Italy. The terrorist grip on the nation relaxed, and labor agitation declined considerably. An important turn-around occurred in 1980 when forty thousand FIAT workers refused to follow their union calls for a strike and marched en masse through the center of Turin. Tired of the state of emergency that had ruled the workplace since the late 1960s, they took a step back, partly replacing union discipline with management's. One victim of the new attitude was the CGIL–UIL–CISL federation that collapsed in 1984. The decline was hastened during the decade by the appearance of smaller independent workers groups, the *Comitati di Base*, or COBAS—grassroots committees, which undercut further the strength of organized labor.

Among Catholics, the election in 1978 of Karol Wojtila as John Paul II, their first Polish pope, heartened many that a new and less experimental era had begun, one more stable than the calamitous years of Paul VI. Italy barely took its breath, however, before new challenges emerged. Led by healthy expansion in central and northeastern Italy, a new prosperity developed that edged the nation into the front rank of the world's consumer nations. The shaky economy of the early and mid-1970s did not last, and, despite the first GNP drop since the war in 1975, Italy's economy expanded at about 3 percent per annum over the decade, better than most of the other industrial leaders. But the good times joined with a new round of scandals and political upheavals to end the regime that had functioned since the fall of Fascism.

DC Power Erodes

As traditional Italy, the Catholic pre-industrial peasant-based *pay reel*, evolved into a secular and consumer nation, Christian Democratic hopes dimmed. The darkened skies came with the decline of the small farmer and peasant class, sectors to which the DC had traditionally appealed and which fell victim to the industrialization and modernization process. Electoral statistics illustrate that the party's support slipped after 1958 to less than 40 percent of the total. For the next twenty-five years, the DC bounced about mostly between 38 and 39 percent depending on the election until 1983 when it hit a low at 32.9 percent.

Change in the political status quo was illustrated in 1981 when the popular Republican Giovanni Spadolini became the first non-DC premier since 1945. The Christian Democrats still controlled the ruling coalition and held most of the ministries, but the time had finally come to end their long dominance.

An assault on the bloated public sector corroded DC influence in the economy and the control of jobs that it had cultivated since the Second World War II, a goldmine made even more impressive thanks to the bureaucratic expansion that accompanied the recent social legislation. Government debt, which had been nonexistent in the boom years of the early 1960s, skyrocketed with the establishment of the welfare state in the 1970s. Social and medical benefits, an enormous pensions list and the gigantic state economy weighed Rome down as its fiscal albatross.

Much of the attack on the lumbering public sector and broad welfare network came from a new breed of reformers of the bare bone, technocrats inspired by the Reagan and Thatcher revolutions in America and Britain and who advocated the same for Italy. Government, they insisted, was too fat, and the impulse to run it like a business led to widespread privatization. Among the chief advocates of this new entrepreneurialism were the Milanese media mogul Silvio Berlusconi and his political ally, Bettino Craxi, who became Italy's first Socialist prime minister in 1983.

One early target of Rome's divestiture was a DC cash cow, the Cassa per il Mezzogiorno, which was axed in 1984. Two years later under the capable management of the Catholic economist Romano Prodi, the job-rich IRI sold Alfa Romeo to FIAT. Other concerns such as Alitalia airlines were later sold off until, in 1999, the IRI, itself, dissolved.

Italy's membership in the European Community, moreover, sped change in the management of the economy. Moribund for much the 1970s and early 1980s, the European Community's acceleration toward a single currency turned serious. In December 1991, Rome agreed to the belt-tightening called for in the Maastricht Treaty that required that government debt be severely reduced and prompted more sale of state-owned concerns and cutbacks in state assistance.

While DC influence over the economy relaxed, so did Catholicism's hold on society. The upheavals that began in the 1960s, the tumultuous "years of the bullet," and the consumer revolution all held social and cultural consequences. Italy was rapidly becoming less Catholic and more secular, less rural and devout and more urban, bourgeois, and modern. As early as 1970, Silvano Burgalassi, a cleric and a scholar, estimated that only 15 percent of Italians were orthodox Catholics. Another 20 percent, he figured, saw Catholicism as folkloric rituals to serve "ancient needs." Five percent were charismatics, 5 percent atheists, and 55 percent had simply become indifferent to the Catholic Church. Catholic Action membership rolls reflected the trend, suffering a dramatic erosion from three million in 1964 to 816,000 in 1973.

In the 1970s, divorce and abortion emerged as the two chief battlefields in the war over secularization. Cognizant of the nihilism of the age, Christian Democracy was happy to ignore the two issues, while the Communists, edging toward the government and anxious to avoid inflammatory and messy confrontations, also soft-peddled the questions. Loris Fortuna, a Socialist deputy, had introduced a modest divorce measure in 1965 to the Chamber of Deputies, but the times were not yet ripe for such a bill and it failed. In 1970, however, she joined with a Liberal, Antonio Baslini, for another try, this time with the help of Panella's Radicals, and was crowned with success.

Effective on December 1, 1970, the law was still rather conservative and required a five-year waiting period (reduced to three years in 1987). Nevertheless, two days after it passed, stunned Catholics formed a National Committee for a Referendum on Divorce to bring the issue to a popular vote. A referendum was finally set for May 12–13, 1974, a date that perhaps allowed too much time for the public to grow accustomed to the new situation. By 1974, 90,000 divorces had been granted and even Catholic ranks started to divide on the issue. In the end, 59.1 percent of the votes sanctioned the right to a divorce, dealing the DC and the church a bitter blow.

A year later Pannella and the *Movimento della Liberazione delle Donne* organized a protest in Rome and a petition drive for a referendum on abortion. Italy had permitted legal contraception only in 1971, and abortion was still a topic rarely discussed in public and certainly not in polite society. Illegal procedures, however, had become fairly common. A compromise passed in 1978 that required a seven-day reflection period before the procedure could be performed, parents' permission for girls under the age of eighteen, and the right of conscientious objection for doctors and nurses (who were often Catholic sisters). Two-thirds of Italy's doctors refused to perform the operation.

As in the divorce precedent, the DC and the church reacted with vigor. A "Movement for Life" immediately formed to defeat abortion in a new referendum. This time the Radicals, too, dissatisfied by what they saw as a tepid law, mobilized for their own referendum that would permit abortion on demand. The DC cause was hampered when it discovered itself in an uncomfortable situation, as an embarrassed ally of the MSI that had joined to support the abortion ban. The DC also weathered church criticism that its proposal was insufficient in allowing for abortion to save the life of the mother. Caught in the middle, the Christian Democrats assembled somewhat timidly behind Pope John Paul II, who campaigned to ban abortion.

When the new pontiff was wounded in an assassination attempt less than one week before the referendum, many were convinced that a sympathy vote would guarantee victory for the Catholic proposal. A Turkish terrorist trained by Soviet conspirators in Bulgaria, Mehmet Ali Agca, shot John Paul II while he appeared in a crowded St. Peter's Square. The pontiff survived, but the shooting had little effect on the referendum: 67.5 percent of the voters rejected the Catholic proposal. The Radical one, however, for abortion on demand, was rejected by an even larger 88.5 percent.

With legalization came a rush to clinics, and abortion figures soon crested in the early 1980s. But they declined almost immediately thereafter, from 16.7 per one thousand women between the ages of fifteen and forty-nine in 1982 to 9.3 in 1996. For women between the ages of fifteen and forty-four, the 1996 figure was 11.4, half the U.S. rate. The year 1982 saw the highest number of legal procedures, 231,308, while, by 1996, that figure dropped to 138,925.

The Catholic setbacks coincided with a decision to examine the formal ties between the Italian state and the church. In 1968, the DC justice minister Guido Gonella had already chaired a committee with the task of revising the 1929 Lateran Accords that still governed relations between the two. In 1976, the panel released to the public its recommendations, which included negotiations for a new concordat that would better guarantee religious freedom and allow less state control of church affairs such as veto power over episcopal nominations or forcing bishops to take a loyalty oath to the republic. Religious instruction was to be maintained in all schools, although exemption from it was made easier. Consequently, talks with the Holy See began in late October 1976 and continued until new accords were reached in 1984 and ratified by Bettino Craxi's government in 1985. Catholicism's status as the state religion ended, although its special place in society was still acknowledged, and a new system awarded to the church 0.8 percent of the value of tax returns.

The Communist Party Collapse

Amid the troubles of political Catholicism, the Communist Party was quietly disintegrating, a victim of the Soviet empire's noisier demise in the late 1980s. Ironically, when the Berlin Wall first came down, PCI headquarters in Rome was jubilant since the party had traveled a long road to distance itself from Moscow.

After the Hungarian uprising in 1956, Palmiro Togliatti had proclaimed a "polycentric" policy to break Italy from the Soviet orbit. Despite such public utterances, however, the PCI continued to receive secret assistance from Moscow well into the 1980s. Enrico Berlinguer continued to question the Soviet ties in a 1971 piece in the PCI paper, *L'Unità*, "Internationalism and Autonomy." The year after his 1972 election as party leader, Berlinguer again used the press, in the pages of the Communist review, *Rinascita*, to propose a "historic compromise" with the DC, agreeing to respect the church and Italy's NATO obligations in exchange for a promotion of his social agenda.

As the Communist Party became less frightening and more willing to compromise, it scored significant electoral gains by uniting loyalists and dissatisfied voters who felt that the DC-led coalitions since the "opening to the Left" had been powerless and without ideas in the face of the era's upheavals. The war in Vietnam also fanned the flames of anti-Americanism in the early 1970s, branding the DC guilty by association. The Communists consequently climbed from 27.1 percent of the vote in the 1972 election to 34.4 in 1976, only four points behind the Christian Democrats. Berlinguer's party had come to within striking distance, and political discourse turned seriously to the historic compromise. One observer wrote that the DC had no choice— "Their regime was collapsing around them, amid economic crisis, financial scandal, incipient terrorism and rampant 'secularization.'"[4]

Preparations began for the DC–PCI arrangement when Giulio Andreotti formed a *monocolore* government on March 11, 1978; but five days later the Red Brigades kidnapped Aldo Moro, and hopes for the compromise floundered. Other causes included an inevitable bureaucratic war over the division of government jobs, and a real war in Afghanistan. There, a Communist coup d'état in April 1978 was followed at the end of 1979 by an unpopular Soviet invasion that increased suspicion in Italy toward the PCI. Many Communist Party members registered their own second thoughts over a deal with the Christian Democrats, and membership figures declined. Had Moro lived, he and Berlinguer might have been able to save the historic compromise, but within a year of his murder the arrangement was effectively dead.

In 1984, Berlinguer met his own premature although natural death, leaving the party to the conservative Alessandro Natta, a man with few ideas beyond steering it back to a pro-Soviet course until he resigned in June 1988. Natta's health troubles were the reason, although the party was sicker than he was, ossified and teetering on the brink of extinction. It groped for an alliance with the dynamic Socialists while it slipped in election after election. That Natta's successor was the vigorous and innovative Achille Occhetto raised many hopes for a revitalized PCI.

Revolution in Eastern Europe, however, immediately confronted the new chief and forced a radical transformation of the PCI into "a new democratic, popular and reforming political movement." It discarded its ominous hammer and sickle logo and replaced it with an inoffensive tree. Even the word "Communist" was discarded. For the lack of something better, the party was briefly dubbed "The Thing" (*La cosa*) until the leadership settled on "The Democratic Party of the Left" (*Partito Democratico della Sinistra*, or PDS). A revolt of the intransigents at the 1991 Party Congress led to a schism and the creation of the "Communist Refoundation" Party, which refused to abandon the old ways and harassed the PDS from the far Left. The PDS survived, however, and in 1994, Occhetto surrendered the reins to his protégé, Massimo D'Alema. From 1998 until 2001, D'Alema even assumed the prime minister's post in a ruling coalition. He subsequently dropped the party name again and replaced it with the simpler "Democrats of the Left."

The Collapse of the System

Ample grease for the state machine has long been a fact of life in Italy. No chronology can locate the birth of large-scale corruption, although it unquestionably debilitated the nation throughout the twentieth century. After World War II, the extraordinary stability of the DC regime fostered a complacent and numbing corruption of job security and government contracts, an illness that started with but extended far past the Christian Democracy. By the century's last decade, its weight was unveiled in the "clean hands" (*mani pulite*) investigation that triggered the crash of the nation's political system. Even as late as 1998, after most of the "clean hands" phenomenon had subsided, the World Bank awarded Italy a 4.6 on its "corruption index," far "ahead" of the United States with 7.5 and Great Britain with a relatively spotless 8.7.

An early warning came in January 1977 when a parliamentary commission approved the prosecution of two cabinet members, the Social Democrat Mario Tanassi and Luigi Gui of the DC, caught in a bribery web that linked Rome to the American Lockheed aircraft corporation. More Lockheed fallout and a number of other imbroglios brewed until June of 1978 when the DC president of Italy, Giovanni Leone, resigned in disgrace. The embarrassments coincided with the divorce defeat to beg introspection among DC leaders. The weary party chairman, Benigno Zaccagnini, was the first to break the ice in an interview with *Panorama* magazine. "It's our fault," he confessed. "The chief motive of our Party's activity has become power, how to get it, how to cultivate it."[5]

Scandals of the 1970s proliferated and magnified into those of the 1980s and 1990s, reaching into all corners of national life. In 1981, a new controversy emerged after a police search of the Florentine Masonic headquarters unearthed the "P-2" conspiracy that linked the Salò veteran, Licio Gelli, to a number of cabinet ministers, the military, Peronista elements in Argentina, and the Vatican. Despite an immediate parliamentary investigation launched by Prime Minister Spadolini, neither the full magnitude nor the whole purpose of the P-2 has been unearthed. One particularly lurid tentacle extended to the Vatican-owned Banco Ambrosiano and its director, Roberto Calvi. The beleaguered bank collapsed on June 17, 1982, one day before the discovery of Calvi's lifeless corpse, dangling from a noose below London's Blackfriars Bridge. Implicated in the sinister events, the American chief of the Holy See's Institute for Religious Works, Reverend Paul Marcinkus, enjoyed Vatican protection before he was transferred to the more tranquil pastures of a suburban Chicago parish.

Neither Christian Democratic misdeeds nor the PCI's Moscow connections brought about the political calamity of the early 1990s. Rather, the gnawing conundrum of political graft came to a head thanks to the insatiable appetite of Bettino Craxi. Secretary of the Socialist Party since 1976, the ambitious young Milanese sought to rejuvenate his moribund organization and expand its base at the expense of ideology. On August 4, 1983, Craxi became Italy's first Socialist prime minister with the support of the Republicans, Social Democrats, Liberals, and Christian Democrats, who still commanded a plurality and served as senior partners. They allowed Craxi to position himself at the public banquet table where his appetite proved boundless and pushed him to gorge on as much of the bureaucracy in as short a time as possible.

Craxi and associates, such as Claudio Martelli and Gianni De Michelis, blatantly flaunted the bounty of office in a fashion never witnessed in their predecessors. Christian Democrats may have been corrupt, but they usually veiled it well behind their staid and family-oriented presence. The Venetian De Michelis, on the other hand, frequented cabarets and discos with an entourage of starlets and models whom he accompanied him the next day at international conferences. An acclaimed expert on fun, De Michelis even authored a guide book to Europe's best night spots.

Despite the excesses and improprieties, Craxi remained in the prime minister's chair until April 1987 when the Christian Democrats resumed their tenure. Nevertheless, the Socialist stayed as a behind-the-scenes player, and, in November 1991, the press reported a Craxi–Andreotti deal (often called the "CAF" to include the DC leader Arnaldo Forlani) to share control over the next five years. But Autumn's optimism cooled in the winter when the rottenness of Craxi's abuses surfaced in the "clean hands" inquest. A February 1992 raid on the Milan office of Mario Chiesa netted evidence that launched the beginning of the end of postwar Italy's political system. Chiesa had been one of Craxi's up-and-coming factotums, a vote-getter, bag man, and extortionist whose $50,000-a-year salary could not explain his $9 million net worth.

The attack on *tangentopoli* (or "bribesville") came from a phalanx of state attorneys led by Antonio Di Pietro, who placed Chiesa in Milan's San Vittore prison, a structure that soon became at least a temporary home for many of the city's leading citizens. In March, Chiesa abandoned his silence and detailed his role in Craxi's world of vice—new information that revealed a pattern and a scope of corruption astonishing by any standards. It was revealed, for instance, that Craxi and Martelli had been receiving money from Calvi and the Banco Ambrosiano ten years before.

Hundreds of politicians and commercial leaders were indicted or arrested in a dizzying campaign that hit across all ranks, from two former mayors of Milan to the PSI foreign minister De Michelis, from the ex-PCI party boss of Turin to the Liberal minister of health Francesco De Lorenzo and the DC minister of finance Giovanni Goria. Some broken figures chose suicide. Two of the unfortunates included the financier Raul Gardini who did so at his Milan home three days after Gabriele Cagliari, the ex-president of ENI, killed himself in his cell at San Vittore. By the end of 1993, 144 parliamentary deputies (out of 630) were under investigation, including 70 Christian Democrats and 51 Socialists.

Many envisioned Di Pietro and the other magistrates as modern Davids striking a blow for freedom against the Goliaths of the Italian state. But others questioned the crusading investigators as figures who misused their power for political ends, disgruntled leftists who overstepped their authority to humble a regime that Communism, for forty years, had failed to do. The magistrates, they argued, often held the accused in prison until they went to trial although the great majority of the defendants won their cases when they finally made it to court.

The clearest example and the most important figure brought to trial was the former prime minister and Christian Democratic pillar, Giulio Andreotti. In the autumn of 1999, however, after years of legal battles based on charges that he conspired with the Mafia to murder, judges cleared Andreotti in two court decisions. In Perugia he was absolved completely, and in Palermo he was released for lack of evidence. Despite the poor prosecutorial record of Di Pietro and his associates, however, the accusations and indictments alone were destructive enough to subvert a grossly corrupt political system.

The damage had been done, and the public took the ball from Di Pietro starting with the April 1992 national elections. The PSI stayed remarkably buoyant dropping less than one point from its 1987 figure of 14.3 percent to 13.6. In its first contest after the fall of the Berlin Wall, the PDS received a sobering 16.1 percent, down from the old PCI's 26.6 percent. The hapless DC dipped below 30 percent for the first time since its triumphs of the 1940s. Two administrative elections in June and November of 1993 then sealed the DC's fate, sending it on a nose dive to 20 percent in June and then to 10 percent.

It had become abundantly clear that Italian politics needed a complete overhaul. The first step took place in 1993 when the renegade Christian Democrat and son of a former Italian president, Antonio Segni, broke with what remained of his party and led a successful referendum campaign for electoral reform. His actions bore fruit that April when 82.7 percent of the voters condemned the system and opted for change.

Parliament responded in 1994 with legislation that jettisoned most of the old proportional system and replaced it with an arrangement for the election of three-quarters of the deputies through a "majoritarian" or "first past the post" method. The other quarter would be sent to Rome the old way. The system proved too clumsy, however, and despite a failed attempt at reform in 2001, further measures appear inevitable.

In March 1994, the first national elections under the new rules produced a legislature that bore little semblance to the old chamber. With 2.2 percent of the tally, the Socialists were eliminated as a force. Craxi had already resigned from the PSI the preceding February and later fled the country, blaming others for his party's troubles from his villa in Tunisia where he died in exile in 2000.

The Christian Democracy voted to disband on January 18, 1994, but while the DC was gone political Catholicism persisted. Some Left-leaning factions resurrected the banner of the pre-Fascist Popular Party (*Partito Popolare Italiano*, or PPI), while conservatives formed the Christian Democratic Center (*Centro Cristiano Democratico*). The former earned 11 percent of the vote in the 1994 vote although it suffered another schism in 1995. The latter joined the ruling Center–Right coalition in 2001 and 2002 when its leader, Pierferdinando Casini, served as president of the Chamber of Deputies.

Catholic Action membership rolls bottomed out and the numbers stabilized. By 2001, it enrolled 386,000, 63 percent of whom (in 1994) were women, still making Catholic Action Italy's largest such organization. Other lay believers regrouped in new, smaller formations such as the Community of Sant'Egidio and Communion and Liberation (*Comunione e Liberazione,* or CL). The Community of Sant'Egidio formed among Rome's *liceo* students in the late 1960s to serve the poor and distressed of the city. In 1973, the group located a monastery and church in the Trastevere quarter to serve as a base, and it received papal sanction in 1986. By then, the Sant'Egidio community had expanded to aid the poor and distressed around the world. By 2002, forty thousand people were affiliated with the community.

With seventy thousand Italian members (it became a world wide society), CL was a larger organization than the Community of Sant'Egidio. Under Don Luigi Giussani, a professor at Milan's Catholic University, it began as groups of Catholic Action student in response to the unrest of the 1960s. By the 1970s, followers coalesced into a militant society to promote traditional Catholic values in a rapidly secularizing Italy. Under the leadership of the philosopher Rocco Buttiglione, the CL then expanded past the university and assumed a place on the national stage.

The culture of Catholicism, furthermore, continued to play a role in the daily lives of Italians. A majority still married in the church, and more than nine out of ten baptized their children as Catholics. Indicators revealed that weekly church attendance actually climbed between 1975 and 1992, from 28.8 percent of the population to 39.4 percent. Another 40 percent attended mass at least a few times during the year, and 7.3 percent went several times a week.

The New Regime

The quagmire of Roman politics gave birth to a new political spectrum that ushered Italy into the twenty-first century. The roster started on the Left with the Communist Refoundation and the Democrats of the Left. In the Center, the Catholic splinter parties waited for a new coalition or union. On the Right, Italy had one vastly reformed old party, the National Alliance, born from the neo-Fascist MSI, and two new creations, Silvio Berlusconi's *Forza Italia* and Umberto Bossi's Northern League.

Perhaps the greatest surprise came in January 1994 when the neo-Fascist MSI transformed itself into the National Alliance (*Alleanza Nazionale*). In 1990, its leader, Gianfranco Fini, had emerged victorious after a three-year power struggle with the old guard hard-liner Pino Rauti. Fini determined that a new name would reflect a detachment from Mussolini's legacy and that the metamorphosis would leave "a great Center–Right pole bringing together people from the MSI, from the Catholic Party and from the lay parties."[6] His load was lightened in that the MSI had wandered alone for over forty years and, ideology aside, could hardly be accused of corruption. More help came from the collapse of DC in the south, passing voters to the National Alliance.

The largest faction among the newcomers was the Forza Italia, a business-oriented conservative party. Its founder was Silvio Berlusconi, a magnate identified most often with his media empire and his AC Milan soccer club. Through his enormous holding company, Fininvest, however, Berlusconi's reach extended much farther in Italy and abroad. A member of the notorious P-2 masonic lodge, he was also a close ally of Bettino Craxi, who stood as best man at Berlusconi's second marriage. His political support surfaced inauspiciously in late 1993 as Forza Italia clubs, but by the March 1994 elections, Forza Italia registered as the nation's most popular party with 21 percent of the vote. Although he served as Italy's prime minister later that year, Berlusconi was convicted in 1998 of bribes to Craxi in 1991. The embarrassment, however, seemed to have had little effect on Forza Italia's or Berlusconi's future electoral prospects. He captured the prime minister's chair for a second time in May of 2001 after his Center–Right coalition scored major successes in regional elections that April.

Umberto Bossi's Northern League began as a protest against corrupt Rome, which, it felt, channeled northern tax money into the pockets of southern politicians. A former medical student from Varese, Bossi was considered something of a crank until the political chaos of the early nineties awarded him a national platform. Inspired by Legnano, the medieval victory of north Italian communes over the German forces of Frederick Barbarossa, Bossi took a cue from an earlier movement in the Veneto to form a League for Lombard Autonomy in 1982. In the 1987 elections, his organization made little impression with 0.4 percent. Five years later, however, he announced his intention to form a Republic of the Po Lands (Padania), which would be a modern, efficient and northern state unencumbered by Roman bureaucracy and debilitated by handouts to southerners.

Enemies condemned Bossi and his followers as xenophobes and perhaps racists, but the league were rarely considered corrupt since, like the MSI, it had never shared power in Rome. Bossi's resentment caught on, and in 1991, he stunned the DC by beating it in its Lombard stronghold of Brescia. A year later in Mantua, Bossi's League and a smaller rival led by his sister captured 40 percent of the vote, while the DC sank to 14 percent and the Socialists to 7 percent. In the 1996 national elections to the Chamber of Deputies, Bossi's League scored an respectable 10.1 percent, almost all of it in the north.

Berlusconi took the prime minister's chair in May 1994 at the head of a Forza Italia—National Alliance—League coalition. Bossi quarreled with the other two leaders, however, and the ministry lasted only until December. After a government of technocrats under Lamberto Dini, a Center–Left cabinet, the "Olive" (*Ulivo*) coalition, formed under the ex-DC economics professor, Romano Prodi. The Center–Left shifted occasionally but formed the basis for all governments through the end of the decade. The Center–Right revival in the regional elections of April 2001 and in Berlusconi's second ministry however, illustrated that politics remained unsettled.

Consumer Nation

At the end of the twentieth century, Italy's economy appeared more and more typical of those found at the top rank of global leaders. It was a charter member in 1974 of the Group of Seven, the world's leading industrial powers, while its integration into the European Community continued apace. By 1997, 60.6 percent of the value of Italy's imports and 54.6 percent of its exports were with fellow members of the European Union. In 1999, thanks to its accommodation to the Maastricht demands, Italy formed part of the euro zone of European currency. The euro officially replaced the lira in January 2002.

Trends at the start of the new century continued to work against jobs in heavy industry and agriculture while favoring such tertiary sectors as transportation and tourism, now Italy's biggest business. By 1997, the State Statistical Institute listed that agriculture occupied only 1,370,000 of the employed labor force. The south, with about one third of Italy's workers, significantly contained about one-half of those in agriculture. Industry far surpassed agriculture, with 6,449,000 employed. Small firms remained a significant component here as 37.4 percent of industrial workers were still found in concerns of fewer than fifty employees. The third sector, however, overwhelmed the other two with a work force of 12,268,000. The elite of this group that the government identified as "professionals, researchers and technicians" almost tripled from 8.7 percent in 1971 to 22.1 percent in 1993. Further down, the amount of managers and office workers engaged in the service sector grew 40.6 percent in the 1980s.

Prosperity continued to smile on the center and north more than it did on the Mezzogiorno, where the "southern question" persisted as a nagging problem. Although the *Cassa* disbanded, Rome and the European Community continued special aid programs and lavished state subsidies on corporations willing to locate there, with limited success. On the positive side, Texas Instruments undertook joint ventures with the Italian government in 1989 and 1996 at Avezzano. At Matera, the "*sassi*" cave dwellings that had humiliated Italy in the 1950s were rediscovered in the 1990s as trendy homes for the gentry. The United Nations enshrined the "*sassi*" as part of the world's cultural patrimony, and at the start of the twenty-first century masons and craftsmen busily renovate them.

But not all of the south shared in Avezzano's and Matera's good fortune, and most of it still waited for a take off. Views of southern terrain still remained marred with the ruins of half-finished or abandoned factory buildings, while double-digit unemployment and low wages continued to limit opportunities for southern families. In 1998, unemployment rates for the mainland south stood at 21.3 percent and 23.3 percent for Sardinia and Sicily. The figure for northeast Italy was 5.1 percent and 6.8 percent for the northwest. The worst regional rate was Calabria's 26.1 percent, while the best was the Trentino/Alto Adige's 3.2 percent.

Food and drink, moreover, continued to occupy more of a southerner's monthly budget than it did for his or her northern cousin. In 1996, the average food bill required 25.6 percent of a Sicilian family's income and 27.1 percent in Apulia. In the north the corresponding figures were 19.3 percent for Piedmont and 18.2 percent in Lombardy.

As a whole, however, through the 1980s and 1990s, more and more Italians enjoyed more and more consumer things. By 1994, 94 percent of Italian families owned color television sets, a good indicator of modern consumption, up from 3 percent only seventeen years before when color TV was new. In 1977, furthermore, almost nobody owned a second set, while in 1994, 64 percent of families did. Here, too, the north–south disparity can be measured. In 1996, 312 sets existed for every 1,000 people in the north and center, while the same number of southerners possessed 220.

Television ownership not only proliferated; program offerings also expanded, a phenomenon that illustrated the entrepreneurial trend in the Italian economy. Judges paved the way for media capitalists in 1976 when the Constitutional Court ruled against the RAI's monopoly of local programming. New forces jumped on the broadcasting scene, launching transmissions that broke the state's grip. The publishing group Rizzoli and the respected Milan journal *Corriere della sera* acquired Telealtomilanese, while Silvio

Berlusconi inaugurated his Telemilano, which became Canale 5 in 1980. Other stations joined them such as Italia 1 of the Rusconi publishing concern and Retequattro, of which Mondadori Publishing held the controlling interest. It was not long, however, before Berlusconi added both to his conglomerate. The government maintained its exclusive control of news programming during the first years of this tele-revolution but ultimately lost it, first to Berlusconi and then to other networks. Gone, too, were the days of effective censorship, and by the mid and late 1980s nudity flourished on mainstream strip shows such as *Colpo grosso*. By 2002, however, it appeared that some of the worst excesses of Italian television had passed.

Other indicators of the consumer revolution can be easily located. One was automobile ownership, which climbed until 1998 when it was discovered that Italians possessed more cars, per capita, than any other people on Earth. The number of foreign vacations, another indicator, doubled for Italians between 1982 and 1993.

The revolution soon hit the Italian ritual of dining. While Italians in the early 1990s ate twice as much meat as they had only twenty-five years before, some of it came from the fast-food monolith, MacDonald's, which launched its first Italian franchise in Rome's swanky Piazza di Spagna in the 1980s. From 1960 to 1990, furthermore, Italians cut their wine consumption almost in half, from an annual average of 106.7 liters per capita to 60.5 liters. Alarmed citizens from all points on the political spectrum banded together to challenge the global economy's assault on their culinary (and cultural) traditions. Their lead vehicle was the Slow Food Movement. Founded in Piedmont in 1986 by Carlo Petrini, the movement expanded into an international phenomenon and from Paris issued a manifesto urging people to "rediscover the richness and aromas of local cuisines, to fight the standardization of Fast Food." But the movement's mascot, the snail, faced an uphill trek. The damage was already done; MacDonald's proliferated, and in 1999 even Dunkin' Donuts opened a Roman outlet that faced onto the Trevi Fountain.

Environmental Concerns

Along with fast food, auto emissions, water pollution, and garbage surfaced as reminders of Italy's material success. An early warning occurred at the Icmesa chemical plant at Seveso near Milan where, on July 10, 1976, an explosion sent a deadly cloud of toxic gas over the area. The state was slow to respond to the poisons, and, although children with skin lesions were admitted to the hospital on the 15th, evacuation of the town began only on the 25th. The unfortunate people of Seveso later bonded with the victims of the 1986 Soviet nuclear disaster at Chernobyl. Elsewhere, chronic concerns over water pollution, furthermore, frequently fell on deaf ears until the predictable beach closings plagued vacationers into the new millennium.

Some responded to the alarm bells and began to display more of an interest in the environment. By the 1980s, older groups such as the Touring Club Italiano and the Club of Rome were joined by new ones such as the Green (*Verde*) Party to lobby for a cleaner Italy. The Greens took their cause to the government and elected their first deputies in 1987. That more attention was paid to the problem meant that state-protected lands tripled between 1984 and 1995, from 963,800 hectares to 2,855,265.

Health and Demographic Issues

A corresponding sensitivity to some personal health issues distinguished Italian society. A personal athletics craze swept Italy in the 1980s and 1990s, and per capita spending on sports became the highest in Europe. The number of smokers who were over fourteen years old sank from 34.9 percent in 1980 to 26.1 percent in 1996. The decline, however, was entirely on the part of men, while women's rates increased slightly during the period. Smoking, moreover, continued to be more of a problem in the Mezzogiorno: 2.1 percent of the average Sicilian's monthly expenditures went for tobacco in 1996, while the figure for his or her cousin in Emilia Romagna was 1.2 percent.

Hard drugs proved another health issue bound with social and moral questions. Through most of the twentieth century, abuse of illegal drugs was almost unheard of and was the stuff of foreigners. Then, in 1973 Italy recorded its first overdose death, the only one of that year. The figures escalated in the 1980s and 1990s until they reached twelve and thirteen hundred per year. The number of addicts in treatment centers also rose, from 22,856 in 1984 to 71,460 in 1992, and, according to Italy's 2000 report to the European Monitoring Center for Drugs and Drug Addiction, the figure reached 142,000. By the new millenium, Italy had joined the unenviable first rank of European nations in per capita drug use.

The new Italy also faced an alarming demographic departure from the old, probably its greatest social dilemma for the foreseeable future. Through the first three-quarters of the century, the nation's birthrate had been higher than most of Europe's, and the large family, while hardly universal, was nevertheless something of a social stereotype. The birth rate, paradoxically, also declined for most of the same period, a problem that Mussolini's family policies recognized but could not halt. Beginning in the 1960s and 1970s, moreover, the rate began to plummet. The average Italian household shrank from 3.3 people in 1971 to an estimated 2.69 people in 1997. Single-resident households increased from 10.6 percent of the total to 21.3 percent, and those with six or more members fell from 14.4 percent to 1.6 percent. By 1995, the fertility rate sank to fewer than 1.2 children per woman, an airtight guarantee of fewer Italians in the future.

Along with the moral and philosophical issues raised in the birthrate collapse, catastrophic consequences loomed for Italy's old age welfare and its bloated pension system. Turn-of-the-century Bologna provided one of the most disturbing illustrations of this, a city with a birthrate of 0.8 percent. Extending the graph lines to about 2020 indicates that for every Bolognese child under five, twenty-five adults would be over fifty. Of those twenty-five, moreover, ten would be at least eighty years old. In 1998, the Catholic sociologist, Pierpaolo Donati, noted in the *New York*

Times, that "It is impossible to have a human society built like this." Bologna's mayor at the time, the ex-Communist Walter Vitali agreed. "Let's face it," he told the reporter, "something is going on here that is very troubling."

The influx of immigrants offset in some measure Italy's birthrate collapse. Official figures in January 1997 listed 884,555 resident foreigners, of which 155,476 lived in Rome and just under 100,000 in Milan. By 2000, unofficial estimates placed these numbers closer to two million legal and illegal residents. The immigrants came mainly from north Africa and Eastern Europe and settled mostly in the north and center, with only 17 percent in the south and islands.

Many Italians reacted anxiously to the newcomers. While Italy contained a much smaller percentage of resident foreigners than did the three other large nations of Europe, public opinion polls illustrated a broader resentment against them than that found in Britain, Germany, or France. In 1994, a Eurobarometer survey revealed that about 52 percent of the French and 60 percent of Italians felt that too many foreigners lived in their countries. The same poll, however, revealed Italians to be less prepared to discriminate and restrict entry.

This was grist for the mills of conservative and right-wing parties and skinheads, but the uneasiness was widespread and genuine. Prime Minister Berlusconi's notorious comment that he felt many of the new immigrants made good servants added to the calls of his government partner, Bossi, to end entry and repatriate many of the newcomers. The Catholic Church expressed an anxiety over aggressive Muslims who might assault Italy's own culture with their ideas and ways of life. That Rome's first mosque was built in the 1990s must have raised eyebrows, and prelates from Bologna's conservative Cardinal Giacomo Biffi to Milan's liberal Carlo Maria Martini worried for Christian and Western European family values in the face of male-dominated Islamic models that vied for a place in twenty-first century Italy. Osama bin Laden's September 11, 2001, attacks on the United States stiffened and heightened Italian anxiety over the Islamic presence in Italy.

Other voices reminded Italians that the demographic crisis made the immigrants necessary to maintain the nation's economic vitality. As a country that had sent immigrants abroad in the past, Italy's history demanded that it now accept others from other places. Cardinal Biffi offered one solution by advocating Italian recruitment of Christian workers from Latin America and the Philippines.

The immigrant challenge, however, was emblematic rather than causal. Immigrants came because Italy's prosperous economy attracted them. It offered them more opportunities than did their homelands, and it drew them almost as much as Germany's or Britain's did. Other perceived problems, such as fast food, arrived in Italy because this same prosperity had created new and authentic demands. Whether with industrialization early in the twentieth century or with the global economy at the end of it, material success, for better or ill, was responsible for many of the cultural laments heard at the dawn of the new millennium.

Notes

1. Robert Lumley, *States of Emergency: Cultures of Revolt in Italy from 1968 to 1978* (London: Verso, 1990), 279–80.
2. Anne Cornelisen, *Women of the Shadows* (Boston: Little, Brown, 1976), 8.
3. Paul Ginsborg, *A History of Contemporary Italy: Society and Politics 1943–1988* (London: Penguin, 1990), 367.
4. Martin Clark, *Modern Italy 1871–1995* (London: Longman, 1996), 387–88.
5. Agostino Giovagnoli, *Il partito italiano: La Democrazia Cristiana dal 1942 al 1994* (Rome-Bari: Laterza, 1996), 169.
6. Patrick McCarthy, *The Crisis of the Italian State from the Origins of the Cold War to the Fall of Berlusconi and Beyond* (New York: St. Martin's Press, 1997), 161.

Bibliography

T O PREPARE A SHORT WORK such as this, the author must sift
through great amounts of information and leave most of it
out. Considering this text as an introductory one, political history
forms the essential skeleton for the rest of the story. Amounts of
economic, social, and cultural history were then applied to
achieve a more complete picture, although most readers with any
background in Italian history will present perfectly reasonable arguments over whether the proper attention was given to this or
that. The following bibliography will hopefully in some measure
redress those anxieties.

This is a partial list of academic books in Italian history that
were either written in English or translated into it. Occasional ref-
erence is made to seminal or fundamental studies that are still
found only in Italian. General studies on modern Italy include
Denis Mack Smith, *Modern Italy: A Political History* (Ann Arbor:
University of Michigan Press, 1997); Martin Clark, *Modern Italy
1871–1995* (1996) in Longman's History of Italy series; Spencer
M. Di Scala, *Italy from Revolution to Republic, 1700 to the Present*
(Boulder, Colo.: Westview, 1998); Roger Absalom, *Italy since 1800:
A Nation in the Balance?* (London: Longman, 1995); and Christo-

pher Duggan, *A Concise History of Italy* (Cambridge: Cambridge University Press, 1994). Also useful are Frank Coppa, ed., *Dictionary of Modern Italian History* (Westport, Conn.: Greenwood, 1985), and Frank Coppa and William Roberts, eds., *Modern Italian History: An Annotated Bibliography* (New York: Greenwood, 1990).

Some of the most enduring works on pre-Fascist Italy are Christopher Seton-Watson, *Italy from Liberalism to Fascism* (London: Methuen, 1967); Salvatore Saladino, *Italy from Unification to 1919: Growth and Decay of a Liberal Regime* (New York: Crowell, 1970); and Benedetto Croce's classic *A History of Italy, 1871–1915* (New York: Atheneum, 1963).

On Giovanni Giolitti, A. William Salomone's *Italy in the Giolittian Era: Italian Democracy in the Making 1900–1914* (Philadelphia: University of Pennsylvania Press, 1960) remains a key work in the prime minister's resurrection. A more recent study by Alexander De Grand, *The Hunchback's Tailor: Giovanni Giolitti and Liberal Italy from the Challenge of Mass Politics to the Rise of Fascism* (Westport, Conn.: Praeger, 2001), is the best biography of the man.

On Nationalists and the pre-Fascist right, see Alexander De Grand, *The Italian Nationalist Association and the Rise of Fascism in Italy* (Lincoln: University of Nebraska Press, 1978). A more general work, Ron Cunsolo's *Italian Nationalism from Its Origins to World War II* (Malabar, Fla.: Kreiger, 1990), includes a section of primary readings. See also Michael Ledeen, *The First Duce: D'Annunzio at Fiume* (Baltimore: Johns Hopkins University Press, 1977).

A valuable overview of the political Left is Alexander De Grand, *The Italian Left in the Twentieth Century* (Bloomington: Indiana University Press, 1989). Spencer Di Scala focuses on Filippo Turati in his *Dilemmas of Italian Socialism* (Boston: University of Massachusetts Press, 1980), which he followed with *Renewing Italian Socialism: Nenni to Craxi* (New York: Oxford University Press, 1988) and *Italian Socialism between Politics and History* (Amherst: University of Massachusetts Press, 1996). James Miller also deals with the issue in his *From Elites to Mass Politics: Italian Socialism in the Giolittian Era, 1900–1914* (Kent, Ohio: Kent State University Press, 1990). Antonio Gramsci has been the subject of a short biography by James Joll, *Antonio Gramsci* (New York: Penguin, 1977), and one by Martin Clark, *Antonio Gramsci and the Revolution That Failed* (New Haven, Conn.: Yale University Press, 1977). The best one in English remains John Cammett's *Antonio Gramsci and the Origins of Italian Communism* (Stanford, Calif.: Stanford University Press, 1967). John Davis has edited a collection of essays on the Communist leader in his *Gramsci and Italy's Passive Revolution* (London: Croom Helm, 1979). Postwar Communism has been examined in Joan Barth Urban's *Moscow and the Italian Communist Party: From Togliatti to Berlinguer* (Ithaca, N.Y.: Cornell University Press, 1986) and a collection of essays edited by Donald L. M. Blackmer and Sidney Tarrow, *Communism in Italy and France* (Princeton, N.J.: Princeton University Press, 1975). David Kertzer discusses the downfall of the Party in his *Politics and Symbols: The Italian Communist Party and the Fall of Communism* (New Haven, Conn.: Yale University Press, 1996).

Church–state relations have been examined by Carlo Jemolo, *Church and State in Italy, 1850–1950* (Oxford: Blackwell, 1960); P. Vincent Bucci, *Chiesa e Stato, Church–State Relations in Italy within the Contemporary Constitutional Framework* (The Hague: Martinus Nijhoff, 1969). Frank Coppa's *The Modern Papacy since 1789* (New York: Longman, 1998) is a general work with special attention paid to Italy. Studies on church–state relations during the Fascist era include John F. Pollard, *The Vatican and Italian Fascism, 1929–1932: A Study in Conflict* (Cambridge: Cambridge University Press, 1985); Peter Kent, *The Pope and the Duce: The International Impact of the Lateran Agreements* (New York: St. Martin's, 1981); and Richard J. Wolff, *Between Pope and Duce: Catholic Students in Fascist Italy* (New York: Lang, 1990). Richard Webster, *Christian Democracy in Italy, 1860–1960* (London: Hollis & Carter, 1961), remains one of the best books on the subject. Michael Patrick Fogarty's general work, *Christian Democracy in Europe, 1820–1953* (South Bend, Ind.: Notre Dame University

Press, 1957), still stands up well, as does Mario Einaudi and Francois Goguel's *Christian Democracy in Italy and France* (South Bend, Ind.: Notre Dame University Press, 1952).

R. J. B. Bosworth contributes a historiographic study of Italian Fascism in his *The Italian Dictatorship: Problems and Perspectives in the Interpretation of Mussolini and Fascism* (London: Arnold, 1998). The best English-language work on the establishment of the Fascist regime is Adrian Lyttleton's *The Seizure of Power: Fascism in Italy 1919–1929* (London: Weidenfeld & Nicolson, 1987). Roland Sarti has edited a collection of essays on the regime, *The Axe Within: Italian Fascism in Action* (New York: New Viewpoints, 1974). David Forgacs has edited another valuable collection on aspects of the regime, *Rethinking Italian Fascism: Capitalism, Populism and Culture* (London: Lawrence & Wishart, 1986). A useful overview of the regime can be found in Alexander De Grand, *Italian Fascism: Its Origins and Development* (Lincoln: University of Nebraska Press, 1982). He also compared the Italian and German regimes in *Fascist Italy and Nazi Germany: The " Fascist" Style of Rule* (London: Routledge, 1995). Studies on specific aspects of the regime include Victoria De Grazia, *The Culture of Consent: Mass Organization of Leisure in Fascist Italy* (Cambridge: Cambridge University Press, 1981); Emilio Gentile, *The Sacralization of Politics in Fascist Italy*, trans. Keith Botsford (Cambridge, Mass.: Harvard University Press, 1996); and Roland Sarti, *Fascism and Industrial Leadership in Italy, 1919–1940: A Study in the Expansion of Private Power under Fascism* (Berkeley: University of California Press, 1974). Philip Cannistraro has edited the useful *Historical Dictionary of Fascist Italy* (Westport, Conn.: Greenwood, 1982).

Denis Mack Smith's *Mussolini: A Biography* (New York: Random House, 1983) remains the standard work in English. Any list of works on Mussolini, however, must include Renzo De Felice's monumental multivolume study that begins with *Mussolini il rivoluzionario (1883–1920)* and continues through the two-part *Mussolini il fascista (1921–1929)*, the two-part *Mussolini il Duce (1929–1939)*, and the three-part *Mussolini l'Alleato*, which were published in Turin by Einaudi between 1965 and 1997. The final unfinished volume was posthumously issued. Other studies of key Fascists include Claudio Segrè, *Italo Balbo: A Fascist Life* (Berkeley: University of California Press, 1987); Harry Fornari, *Mussolini's Gadfly: Roberto Farinacci* (Nashville: Vanderbilt University Press, 1971); and Ray Moseley, *Mussolini's Shadow: The Double Life of Galeazzo Ciano* (New Haven, Conn.: Yale University Press, 2000). An essential memoir of the Fascist era, however, comes from the foreign minister's own hand: *The Ciano Diaries 1939–1943: The Complete Unabridged Diaries of Count Galeazzo Ciano, Italian Minister of Foreign Affairs, 1936–1943*, ed. Hugh Gibson (New York: Fertig, 1973).

General studies of fascism as an international idea with specific references to Italy include Stanley Payne, *A History of Fascism, 1914–1945* (Madison: University of Wisconsin Press, 1995); Roger Eatwell, *Fascism: A History* (New York: Penguin, 1997); Alan Cassels, *Fascism* (Arlington Heights, Ill.: Harlan Davidson, 1975); and Walter Laqueur, *Fascism: A Reader's Guide* (Berkeley: University of California Press, 1978). Some of the most discussed interpretations of fascism include Ernst Nolte's *The Three Faces of Fascism* (New York: Rinehart & Winston, 1965), a comparison of the Italian model, Nazi Germany, and the Action Française movement in France; Zeev Sternhell et al., *The Birth of Fascist Ideology* (Princeton, N.J.: Princeton University Press, 1994); and Nicos Poulantzas, *Fascism and Dictatorship: The Third International and the Problem of Fascism* (London: Verso, 1979), for a Marxist perspective. A. James Gregor attempts to link fascism and modernism in his *The Ideology of Fascism: The Rationale of Totalitarianism* (New York: Free Press, 1969) and in his *Italian Fascism and Developmental Dictatorship* (Princeton, N.J.: Princeton University Press, 1979). Michael Ledeen studies the attempt by the fascists themselves to organize in his *Universal Fascism: The Theory and Practice of the Fascist International, 1928–1936* (New York: Fertig, 1972).

On the military, the era of World War II is treated in John Whittam, *The Politics of the Italian Army, 1861–1918* (London: Croom Helm, 1977), and John Gooch, *Army State and Society in Italy,*

1870–1915 (Basingstoke, U.K.: Macmillan, 1989). On its performance, see John R. Schindler's *Isonzo: The Forgotten Sacrifice of the Great War* (Westport, Conn.: Praeger, 2001). John Sweet's *Iron Arm: The Mechanization of Mussolini's Army, 1920–1940* (Westport, Conn.: Greenwood, 1980), focuses in useful detail on tanks (*carri armati*). James MacGregor Knox has published two admirable studies of Fascist Italy at war in his *Mussolini Unleashed 1939–1941: Politics and Strategy in Fascist Italy's Last War* (Cambridge: Cambridge University Press, 1982) and *Hitler's Italian Ally: Royal Armed Forces, Fascist Regime and the War of 1940–1943* (Cambridge: Cambridge University Press, 2000). J. J. Sadkovitch examines the navy in *The Italian Navy in World War II* (Westport, Conn.: Greenwood, 1994). Gooch, Knox, and Brian Sullivan also contribute essays on the armed forces during, respectively, World Wars I and II and the interwar period in the three-volume *Military Effectiveness*, ed. Alan R. Millett and Williamson Murray (Boston: Allen & Unwin, 1988).

Key works in English on the persecution of the Jews in Italy are Meir Michaelis, *Mussolini and the Jews: German-Italian Relations and the Jewish Question in Italy 1922–1945* (Oxford: Clarendon, 1978); Renzo De Felice *The Jews in Fascist Italy*, trans. Robert Miller (New York: Enigma, 2001); Alexander Stille, *Benevolence and Betrayal: Five Italian Jewish Families under Fascism* (New York: Summit, 1991); and Susan Zuccotti, *The Italians and the Holocaust* (New York: Basic Books, 1987). Zuccotti's *Under His Very Windows: The Vatican and the Holocaust in Italy* (New Haven, Conn.: Yale University Press, 2000) is one of an avalanche of works dealing generally with the subject although its value here is its focus on Italy. A broader account of Jewish life is found in H. Stuart Hughes, *Prisoners of Hope: The Silver Age of Italian Jews, 1924–1974* (Cambridge, Mass.: Harvard University Press, 1983).

On anti-Fascism, Charles Delzell, *Mussolini's Enemies: The Italian Anti-Fascist Resistance* (Princeton, N.J.: Princeton University Press, 1961), remains essential. See also Frank Rosengarten, *The Italian Anti-Fascist Press, 1919–1945* (Cleveland: Case Western Reserve University Press, 1968); and Stanislao Pugliese, *Carlo Rosselli: Socialist Heretic and Antifascist Exile* (Cambridge, Mass.: Harvard University Press, 1999).

Among the chief studies of the Italian colonial experience is Claudio Segrè's work on Libya, *The Fourth Shore* (Chicago: University of Chicago Press, 1974). Robert Hess discusses Somalia in his *Italian Colonialism in Somalia* (Chicago: University of Chicago Press, 1966). The bulk of colonial literature concerns Ethiopia and includes Angelo Del Boca, *The Ethiopian War, 1935–1941*, trans. P. D. Cummins (Chicago: University of Chicago Press, 1969); Alberto Sbacchi, *Legacy of Bitterness: Ethiopia and Fascist Italy, 1935–1941* (Lawrenceville, N.J.: Red Sea, 1997); and Haile Larebo, *The Building of an Empire: Italian Land Policy and Practice in Ethiopia, 1935–1941* (Oxford: Clarendon, 1994).

The end of World War II is addressed in David W. Ellwood's *Italy 1943–1945* (Leicester, U.K.: Leicester University Press, 1985), a condensed version of his Italian work, *L'Alleato nemico*, which deals with "the politics of war" after Mussolini's fall from power in 1943. See also Steven White, *Progressive Renaissance: America and the Reconstruction of Italian Education, 1943–1962* (New York: Garland, 1991). Jonathan Dunnage has edited *After the War: Violence, Justice, Continuity and Renewal in Italian Society* (London: Troubador, 1999) from papers presented at a University of Sussex conference. John Davis has edited a much larger collection of papers, *Italy and America, 1943–1944* (Naples: Città del Sole, 1997), drawn on a conference at the University of Connecticut. Paul Ginsborg, *A History of Contemporary Italy: Society and Politics 1943–1988* (London: Penguin, 1990), is the best English-language general history of postwar Italy. It was updated, greatly expanded, and released in Italian as *Storia d'Italia 1943–1996: Famiglia, società, stato* (Turin: Einaudi, 1998). Another concise one-volume work is Silvio Lanaro, *Storia dell'Italia repubblicana: L'economia, la politica, la cultura, la società dal dopoguerra agli anni '90* (Venice: Marsilio, 1996). Norman Kogan's *A Political History of Italy: The Postwar Years* (New York: Praeger, 1983) remains one of the most reliable political outlines of the period. Patrick McCarthy edited a more general collection of essays on *Italy since 1945* (New York: Oxford University Press, 2000), part of the Short Oxford History of Italy series.

On the political violence of the "years of the bullet," see Robert Lumley, *States of Emergency: Cultures of Revolt in Italy from 1968 to 1978* (London: Verso, 1990), and Richard Drake, *The Revolutionary Mystique and Terrorism in Contemporary Italy* (Bloomington: Indiana University Press, 1989). On the Right, see Richard Collin, *The De Lorenzo Gambit: The Italian Coup Manqué of 1964* (Beverly Hills, Calif.: Sage, 1977); Franco Ferraresi, *Threats to Democracy: The Radical Right in Italy after the War* (Princeton, N.J.: Princeton University Press, 1996); and essays on Italian neo-Fascism included in Luciano Cheles et al., *The Far Right in Western and Eastern Europe* (New York: Longman, 1995). The Aldo Moro case has been examined in Robin Erica Wagner-Pacifici's *The Moro Morality Play: Terrorism as Social Drama* (Chicago: University of Chicago Press, 1986) and in Richard Drake's *The Moro Murder Case* (Cambridge, Mass.: Harvard University Press, 1995).

The body of works on Italian social and labor history is richer on the pre-1945 period than on the postwar nation. David Kertzer portrays rural life in his *Family Life in Central Italy 1880–1910: Sharecropping, Wage Labor and Co-Residence* (New Brunswick, N.J.: Rutgers University Press, 1984). Turn-of-the-century Milan is dealt with in Louise Tilly's *Politics and Class in Milan, 1881–1901* (New York: Oxford University Press, 1992) and, in a broader and comparative sense, her book with Richard Tilly, *The Rebellious Century, 1830–1930* (Cambridge, Mass.: Harvard University Press, 1975). Donald Bell discusses life in Milan's industrial suburbs in his *Sesto San Giovanni: Workers Culture and Politics in an Italian Town, 1880–1922* (New Brunswick, N.J.: Rutgers University Press, 1980). Anthony Cardoza examines the upper ranks in two works, *Agrarian Elites and Italian Fascism: The Province of Bologna, 1901–1926* (Princeton, N.J.: Princeton University Press, 1982) and *Aristocrats in Bourgeois Italy: The Piedmontese Nobility 1861–1930* (New York: Cambridge University Press, 1997). Frank

Snowden discusses class struggle in his *Violence and the Great Estates of Southern Italy: Apulia, 1900–1922* (New York: Cambridge University Press, 1986) and *The Fascist Revolution in Tuscany 1919–1922* (New York: Cambridge University Press, 1989). Other regional and local studies include those by Walter Adamson, *Avant-Garde Florence: From Modernism to Fascism* (Cambridge, Mass.: Harvard University Press, 1993); Paul Corner, *Fascism in Ferrara, 1915–1925* (London: Oxford University Press, 1975); and Alice Kelikian, *Town and Country under Fascism: The Transformation of Brescia, 1915–1926* (Oxford: Oxford University Press, 1986). Luisa Passerini has contributed a groundbreaking oral history, *Fascism in Popular Memory: The Cultural Experience of the Turin Working Class* (Cambridge: Cambridge University Press, 1987).

On the problem of organized crime, see Pino Arlacchi, *Mafia, Peasants and Great Estates. Society in Traditional Calabria* (Cambridge: Cambridge University Press, 1983); Anton Blok, *The Mafia of a Sicilian Village 1860–1960* (Prospect Heights, Ill.: Waveland, 1988); Christopher Duggan, *Fascism and the Mafia* (New Haven, Conn.: Yale University Press, 1989); and Alexander Stille, *Excellent Cadavers: The Mafia and the Death of the First Italian Republic* (New York: Vintage, 1995).

Luisa Passerini's *Autobiography of a Generation: Italy 1968* (Hanover, N.H.: University Press of New England, 1996) unites oral history with postwar issues. Some interesting information, moreover, can be drawn from Arthur Marwick's comparative volume, *The Sixties* (Oxford: Oxford University Press, 1998). Postwar studies of rural life are often based as much in the social sciences as they are in history. Among the more historically minded of these are Douglas R. Holmes, *Cultural Disenchantments: Worker Peasantries in Northeast Italy* (Princeton, N.J.: Princeton University Press, 1989), and J. Davis, *Land and Family in Pisticci* (New York: Humanities, 1973). Helpful statistical illustrations of contemporary society include Alberto Martinelli, Antonio Chiesi, and Sonia Stefanizzi, *Recent Social Trends in Italy 1960–1995* (Montreal: McGill-Queen's University Press, 1999), and Paolo Natale, ed., *Abacus: Italia al macroscopio* (Milan: Feltrinelli, 1998).

Women as an object of study have received increasing attention, particularly those under Fascism. The definitive work on women and the regime is Victoria de Grazia, *How Fascism Ruled Women: Italy 1922–1945* (Berkeley: University of California Press, 1992). Robin Pickering-Iazzi has edited another work, *Mothers of Invention: Women, Italian Fascism and Culture* (Minneapolis: University of Minnesota Press, 1995). Brian Sullivan and Philip Cannistraro have contributed a study of Margherita Sarfatti in their *Il Duce's Other Woman* (New York: Morrow, 1992). A work on an earlier period is Mary Gibson's *Prostitution and the State in Italy, 1860–1915* (Columbus: Ohio State University Press, 2000). For the postwar period, Anne Cornelisen discusses southern women in *Women of the Shadows* (Boston: Little, Brown, 1976).

Along with the updated Ginsborg study, works published through the 1990s that deal with Italy's still-unresolved political turmoil include Mark Gilbert, *The Italian Revolution: The End of Politics, Italian Style?* (Boulder, Colo.: Westview, 1995); *The New Italian Republic: From the Fall of the Berlin Wall to Berlusconi*, ed. Stephen Gundle and Simon Parker (London: Routledge, 1996); Patrick McCarthy, *The Crisis of the Italian State: From the Origins of the Cold War to the Fall of Berlusconi and Beyond* (New York: St. Martin's, 1997); David Kertzer and Mario Caciagli, eds., *Italian Politics: The Stalled Transition* (Boulder, Colo.: Westview, 1996); Vittorio Bufacchi and Simon Burgess, eds., *Italy since 1989: Events and Interpretations* (New York: St. Martin's, 1998); and a controversial volume by Stanton Burnett and Luca Mantovani, *The Italian Guillotine: Clean Hands and the Overthrow of Italy's First Republic* (Lanham, Md.: Rowman & Littlefield, 1998). Each volume is obviously limited by its publication date.

The special condition of the Mezzogiorno has attracted much academic interest. The second volume of Denis Mack Smith's history of Sicily, *Modern Sicily after 1713* (New York: Dorset, 1968), chronicles events there until the 1960s. An account of Achille Lauro's Naples is Percy Allum, *Politics and Society in Post-War*

Naples (Cambridge: Cambridge University Press, 1973). Jane and Peter T. Schneider's *Culture and Political Economy in Western Sicily* (New York: Academic Press, 1976) examines Sicilian problems in a framework of the social sciences. It was followed by their *Festival of the Poor: Fertility Decline and the Ideology of Class in Sicily 1860–1980* (Tucson: University of Arizona Press, 1996). Recent and more general discussions of the south include *The New History of the Italian South: The Mezzogiorno Revisited* (Exeter: University of Exeter Press, 1997), ed. Robert Lumley and Jonathan Morris, and *Italy's "Southern Question": Orientalism in One Country* (New York: Berg, 1998), ed. Jane Schneider.

On foreign affairs, see R. J. B. Bosworth, *Italy in the Wider World, 1860–1960* (New York: Routledge, 1996). Bosworth also focused on the diplomacy of Giovanni Giolitti and his foreign minister, Di San Giuliano, in *Italy, the Least of the Great Powers: Italian Foreign Policy before the First World War* (Cambridge: Cambridge University Press, 1979). The interwar period has been chronicled by H. James Burgwyn in his *The Legend of the Mutilated Victory: Italy, the Great War, and the Paris Peace Conference, 1915–1919* (Westport, Conn.: Greenwood, 1993) and his *Italian Foreign Policy in the Interwar Period, 1918–1940* (Westport, Conn.: Praeger, 1997). Fascist expansionism was the subject of Denis Mack Smith's *Mussolini's Roman Empire* (Harmondsworth, U.K.: Penguin, 1977) and, in a comparative context, Aristotle Kallis, *Fascist Ideology: Territory and Expansionism in Italy and Germany, 1922–1945* (London: Routledge, 2000), and James Macgregor Knox, *Common Destiny: Dictatorship, Foreign Policy and War in Fascist Italy and Nazi Germany* (Cambridge: Cambridge University Press, 2000). F. W. Deakin examines Fascist Italy's relations with Nazi Germany in his *The Brutal Friendship: Mussolini, Hitler and the Fall of Italian Fascism* (New York: Harper & Row, 1962). Deakin revised the third section of this work and focuses on the Salò period in *The Six Hundred Days of Mussolini* (New York: Doubleday, 1966). Mario Toscano's *Designs in Diplomacy: Pages from European Diplomatic History in the Twentieth Century* (Baltimore: Johns Hopkins University Press, 1970) contains useful essays, and his *The Origins of the Pact of Steel* (Baltimore: Johns Hopkins University Press, 1968) remains among the most reliable books on the subject.

On Italy's foreign relations since World War II, see Norman Kogan, *The Politics of Italian Foreign Policy* (New York: Praeger, 1963); F. Roy Willis, *Italy Chooses Europe* (New York: Oxford University Press, 1971); and Ennio Di Nolfo's edited work, *The Atlantic Pact Forty Years Later: A Historical Reappraisal* (Berlin: Walter de Gruyter, 1991). U.S.–Italian relations have been treated in H. Stuart Hughes, *The United States and Italy* (Cambridge, Mass.: Harvard University Press, 1965), although the work is more far-ranging than its title implies; and James Edward Miller, *The United States and Italy, 1940–1950: The Politics of Diplomacy and Stabilization* (Chapel Hill: University of North Carolina Press, 1986), and, in a comparative sense, in Alessandro Brogi's *A Question of Self-Esteem: The United States and the Cold War Choices in France and Italy, 1944–1958* (Westport, Conn.: Praeger, 2002). Anglo-Italian relations serve as the subject of Moshe Gat's *Britain and Italy, 1943–1949: The Decline of British Influence* (Brighton, U.K.: Sussex Academic Press, 1996). Ennio Di Nolfo also edited a collection of studies, *Power in Europe? Great Britain, France, Germany, and Italy and the Origins of the EEC, 1952–1957* (Berlin: Walter de Gruyter, 1992).

On economics, Shepard B. Clough, *The Economic History of Modern Italy* (New York: Columbia University Press, 1964), is still valuable. The postwar decades were dealt with specifically in George H. Hildebrand's *Growth and Structure in the Economy of Modern Italy* (Cambridge, Mass.: Harvard University Press, 1965). More recent works include Douglas Forsyth's *The Crisis of Liberal Italy 1914–1922* (Cambridge: Cambridge University Press, 1993); John Lamberton Harper's *America and the Reconstruction of Italy, 1945–1948* (Cambridge: Cambridge University Press, 1986); and Vera Zamagni's *The Economic History of Italy, 1860–1990* (Oxford: Clarendon, 1997).

On culture, David Forgasc's *Italian Culture in the Industrial Era* (Manchester, U.K.: Manchester University Press1990) provides an original and extensive view. An early work on Italian culture under the Fascists was Edward R. Tannenbaum, *The Fascist Experience: Italian Society and Culture, 1922–1945* (New York: Basic Books, 1972). The study has been followed by Marla Stone, *The Patron State: Culture and Politics in Fascist Italy* (Princeton, N.J.: Princeton University Press, 1998), Ruth Ben-Ghiat, *Fascist Modernities, Italy 1922–1945* (Berkeley: University of California Press, 2001); and Simonetta Falasca-Zamponi, *Fascist Spectacle: The Aesthetics of Power in Mussolini's Italy* (Berkeley: University of California Press, 2000). Film has been treated in such works as Pierre Leprohon, *The Italian Cinema* (New York: Praeger, 1972); Peter Bondanella, *Italian Cinema from Neo-Realism to the Present* (New York: Ungar, 1983); Mira Liehm, *Passion and Defiance: Film in Italy from 1942 to the Present* (Berkeley: University of California Press, 1984); and Pierre Sorlin, *Italian National Cinema, 1896–1996* (London: Routledge, 1996). Stephen Gundle addresses the film question from the Communist perspective in his *Between Hollywood and Moscow: The Italian Communist Party and the Challenges of Mass Culture* (Durham, N.C.: Duke University Press, 2000). Postwar Italian culture in a more general sense is discussed in a number of essay collections edited by Zygmunt G. Baranski and Robert Lumley, *Culture and Conflict in Postwar Italy* (New York: St. Martin's, 1990); by Christopher Duggan and Christopher Wagstaff, *Italy in the Cold War: Politics, Culture and Society 1948–1958* (Oxford: Berg, 1995); and by David Forgacs and Robert Lumley, eds., *Italian Cultural Studies: An Introduction* (Oxford: Oxford University Press, 1996). Finally, Gino Moliterno has edited a useful *Encyclopedia of Contemporary Italian Culture* (New York: Routledge, 2000).

Index

178   *Index*

Quadrumviri, 53

Racial Laws, 73
Radical Party (*Partito Radicale*), 131, 133, 136, 137
Radio, 55, 56, 115
Rahn, Rudolf von, 86
RAI (Radio Audizioni Italiane), 115, 132, 149
Ratti, Achille. *See* Pius XI
Rauti, Pino, 146
Ravenna, 44
Reagan, Ronald, 135
Red Brigades (Brigate Rosse, BR), 5, 128–31, 139
Red Shirts. *See* Garibaldi, Giuseppe
Red Week, 25
Reggio nell'Emilia, 36
Il Regno, 26
Regno del Sud. See Kingdom of the South
Repubblica Sociale Italiana (RSI). *See* Italian Social Republic
Rerum novarum, 16
Resistance, armed, 79, 89–92, 103
Respighi, Ottorino, 54–55
Il Resto del carlino, 40
Ribbentrop, Joachim, 74–75
Rimini, 91
Rinascita, 138
Risorgimento, 1–3, 5–9, 19
Rivolta femminile. *See* Female Revolt
Rivolta ideale, 26
Rizzoli Publishers, 149
Roatta, Mario, 70, 72
Rocco, Alfredo, 26, 47, 51
Romagna, 25, 44
Roman Question, 15, 57, 59
Rome, 1, 6, 8, 13, 14, 17, 38, 44–45, 54, 58, 61, 80–81, 83, 84, 86–87, 89, 100, 114, 115–16, 126–27, 128, 129–30, 145, 150
Romita, Giuseppe, 100
Rommel, Irwin, 79

Roncalli, Angelo. *See* John XXIII
Roosevelt, Franklin Delano, 77, 105
Rosselli, Carlo and Sandro, 49, 79
Rossellini, Roberto, 56, 116
Rossoni, Edmondo, 44, 53
Royal Academy, 54
Royal House. *See* Savoy
RSI. *See* Italian Social Republic
Ruini, Meiuccio, 97
Rumor, Mariano, 99
Rusconi Publishers, 150
Russia, 25, 26, 34, 36, 40. *See also* Soviet Union
Russian Revolution, 34, 36

Salandra, Antonio, 24, 25, 26, 28, 45
Salerno, 83
Salò. *See* Italian Social Republic
Salvemini, Gaetano, 9, 49
Sant'Egidio, Community of, 144–45
Saraceno, Pasquale, 112
Saragat, Giuseppe, 105, 107, 109
Sardinia, 4, 6, 11
Sarfatti, Margherita, 63
Sarto, Giuseppe. *See* Pius X
Savoy (*Savoia*), 7, 100–102
Scappi, Bartolomeo, 3
Scelba, Mario, 103, 110, 117
Schuschnigg, Kurt, 71
Schuster, Idelfonso, 62, 99
Sciascia, Leonardo, 117
Scoccimarro, Mauro, 100
Sculpture, 19
Second Vatican Council, 120, 125
Segni, Antonio, 144
Selassie, Haile, 61, 69, 78
Seven Weeks War, 8
Severini, Gino, 19
Seveso, 151
Sforza, Carlo, 49, 109
Siccardi Laws, 13
Sicily, 4, 6, 7, 11, 20, 80, 127, 128
Sila Law, 112

About the Author

ROY PALMER DOMENICO is an associate professor of history at the University of Scranton. His publications include *The Regions of Italy: A Reference Guide to History and Culture* (Westport, Conn.: Greenwood, 2002) and *Italian Fascists on Trial, 1943–1948* (Chapel Hill: University of North Carolina Press, 1991), which won the 1992 Helen and Howard R. Marraro Prize from the Society for Italian Historical Studies and which was translated into Italian in 1996.